The Ailing Capitalism

Complimentary copy
for ~~D~~ Shabbar Dhalla.
From: Dr. Mahmood Y. Abdulla.

The Ailing Capitalism

History of Global Stock Market Crashes

Dr. Mahmood Yoosuf Abdulla

A Cataloguing-in-Publication Data entry for this title is available from the British Library.

ISBN-13: 9781530577989
ISBN-10: 1530577985
Library of Congress Control Number: 2016907393
CreateSpace Independent Publishing Platform
North Charleston, South Carolina

CONTENTS

ABOUT THE AUTHOR

Dr. Mahmood Yoosuf Abdulla earned his master of arts from Portsmouth University and a PhD from Loughborough University in the United Kingdom. Awarded the Diploma with Distinction Award in freelance writing from the London School of Journalism, the author has spent the past thirty-five years of his career as a fellow of the Association of Chartered Certified Accountants in London.

The Ailing Capitalism is based on his award-winning academic study.

Dr. Abdulla worked for ten years on World Bank–funded major agricultural-development projects in the Middle East in the advisory capacity of financial expert.

He also worked in public practice, commerce, and industry. He banks on his professional experience in identifying the negative repercussions of the modern-day financial and investment world. He taught postgraduate students at Birkbeck, University of London, in 2007–8 and at the Islamic Institute for Postgraduate Studies, a community organization affiliated with Winchester University in the United Kingdom where he was appointed executive dean in 2009.

Public speaking is his main hobby, which has greatly contributed in his extensive travels, as an invitee to 80 community organizations in 51 cities in Asia, Africa, Europe, North America and Canada, during the past 45 years. He has visited New York alone eight times. He often remarks to his friends: "This city never ceases to fascinate me. It is like being on a new planet altogether."

LIST OF ACRONYMS

BCCI	Bank of Credit and Commerce International
CATS	Computer Assisted Trading System
CDO	Collateralized debt obligation
CD	Certificate of deposit
CDS	Credit default swap
DJIA	Dow Jones Industrial Average
EMT	Efficient market theory
ETO	Exchange-trade option
FSA	Financial Services Authority
FTSE	Financial Times Stock Exchange index (pronounced "footsie")
GCC	Gulf Cooperation Council
GDP	Gross domestic product
HE	The Hutchinson Encyclopedia
IFS	Institute for Fiscal Studies (UK)
IMF	International Monetary Fund
LSE	London Stock Exchange
NASD	National Association of Securities Dealers
NASDAQ	National Association of Securities Dealers Automated Quotations
NBK	the New Book of Knowledge
NINJA	No income, no job, no assets (a type of loan)
NYSE	New York Stock Exchange
OPEC	Organization of Petroleum Exporting Countries
P/E	Price-earnings ratio
RBS	Royal Bank of Scotland

S&L	Savings and loan association
SEAQ	Stock Exchange Automated Quotation system
SEC	Securities and Exchange Commission (United States)
SETS	Stock Exchange Electronic Trading System
TARP	Troubled Assets Relief Program
TSE	Tokyo Stock Exchange

INTRODUCTION

A conscientious observer and researcher of contemporary events would not have escaped observing the upheavals and violent tremors on the global financial and stock markets that have left indelible scars on the lives of many people, especially old-aged pensioners and small investors whose lifetime savings and investments have vanished. Despite rock-solid legislation and rules governing the financial world in the West, financial and stock markets are infested with crooks who operate with confidence to the extent that even if their wrongdoings or financial crimes are discovered, they walk free with the booty they have gained through wrong advice, misrepresentation of facts, and fraud. This study seeks to demonstrate the fact that one of the principal features of the present-day financial world is breach of trust.

The global economic and financial crisis, with acrimonious effects on investors in the stock market, is not a new scenario. Investors entering the market for the first time may not be aware of its history and its short-term and long-term devastations. Despite the tightening of the noose around the main players in the stock market in the form of mountains of legislations, bylaws, rules, and regulatory regimes, abuse has continued unabated, resulting in crises that keep on repeating themselves in cyclical fashion.

It has taken me several years to accumulate material, facts, and figures to embark on this project, which will be of great benefit to unaware and misinformed investors. I have imbued my research files with analytical statistics and data from companies quoted on the London Stock Exchange (LSE) and foreign stock exchanges. This study raises several questions about why anybody, despite being in a fiduciary relationship or position of trust with investors, would be vigilant and prudent in all honesty with money that does not belong to them. The question of abiding by moral and ethical standards does not arise; the only language understood in the world of finance is that of self-interest and insatiable greed, at the expense of innocent members of the public. Never mind the standards—if the fear of legislative controls is removed, even the fireproof vaults of the banks and investment houses will prove to be totally unsafe.

An inquirer has to see beyond superficiality. Sometimes he or she has to dig up old graves, as I have done in this study, even though the odor may be very offensive and sometimes unbearable. The recent menace in the financial world has been caused by those whose covetousness remains unsatisfied, despite their earning staggering multimillions in salaries, bonuses, share-option schemes, pensions, golden handshakes, and compensation schemes. They treat members of the public as sacrificial cows for filling the coffers of their organizations or institutions.

Fraud: A Major Cause of Economic Collapse

In every scandal and fraud, whether it is revealed to the public or remains concealed, public interest gets trampled. For every single million pocketed by a stockbroker or derivative trader, public interest is sacrificed. In every stock market crash, public interest is crushed under the rubble of abuses. The negligence of bankers and supervisory authorities adversely affects public interest. The public is not the beneficiary as much as it is the benefactor of the system, which has never been just and fair to the public. If not for the fear of being caught breaching the law, the corruption prevailing in the system is capable of producing greedy wolves that can tear apart the flesh of the public and feed on its blood.

The laborious work performed by a mason, bricklayer, plumber, garbage collector, or even sewage cleaner is tangible and productive. For every pound or dollar they have earned and saved, they have sweated. If they contribute to a pension scheme or if they invest in insurance or mutual funds, that is because at the end of the day, they want to retire and enjoy their retirement without hassle and worries. But in every financial crisis, many, if not most, pensioners are subject to mental torture simply because the financial institutions or banks they entrusted their savings have literally gambled with their investment money and badly lost. This does not affect the fat cats sitting in the cozy atmosphere of their offices in a skyscraper in Manhattan as much as it affects poor laborers or even white-collar workers who have worked for every cent they have earned. The fact that members of the public are prepared to sacrifice their earned income from their own labor and expertise for a rosy promise to earn unearned income like interest and dividends speaks volumes about the trickery and psychological bombardment of the corporate world in general, and the world of finance in particular, to prey on the public's lack of awareness.

The investment schemes being marketed to the public are so complex in nature that even the computer programmers and analysts responsible for the models get muddled. As a result, the public takes the blows from two sides. On the one hand, investors are likely to lose their earned income, sacrificing it for the sake of unearned income. On the other hand, they are likely to end up with debts and liabilities. Regardless of whether a corporation someone has invested in is earning a decent dividend for shareholders or eating away their equity, as termites eat away wood, the fat cats sitting in their skyscrapers overlooking the Statue of Liberty are unlikely to be moved by the shareholders' plight. They are likely to continue charging them a dollar for every breath they take. Thousands of opportunists are making a living out of the misinformation, unawareness, and misery of the public in all the major financial centers of the world.

Although the stock market is the backbone of interest-based capitalism situated in the open-market economy, its vulnerability and sensitivity can result in destructive effects to the economy. This discourse critically explores the role of derivatives; corporate governance; debt crises in a global economy; corporate fraud; the role of stockbrokers, traders, and speculators; and other issues relevant to the subject matter.

One of the most serious challenges undermining the credibility of the financial world is that of widespread fraudulent dealings. Fraud has acquired professionalism. Fraudulent dealings are not a specialty of the sophisticated financial system in the West only; they have proliferated in developing economies too.

KPMG, a global network of professional service firms, in its 2008 Gulf Cooperation Council (GCC) fraud survey conducted in Manama, the capital of Bahrain, arrived at grim findings. The poll showed that 43 percent believed that fraud was a major problem, and 60 percent maintained that it was set to increase in the region. The survey revealed that losses resulting from financial crimes in the region were likely to run into billions of dollars per annum. Respondents to the survey reported individual losses of some \$100 million. "The survey indicates that fraud perpetrated by management and employees accounted for the bulk of fraud incidents."[1] Thus, the very hands that are entrusted with clients' money are dipped in their blood.

In the West, a number of firms are known to have been involved in making under-the-table payments to corrupt executives in developing countries to win business contracts. Worse than that is the process of opening a representative office in a financial center from where certain dubious investment funds are promoted and marketed through glossy and attractive brochures. Many such funds are incorporated in unregulated offshore financial centers like the Cayman and Cook Islands, although their management may well be based in Britain or America. As soon as the investment funds succeed in attracting enough capital from uninformed and naïve investors, the investment funds and their managers disappear into oblivion.

It is claimed that at least ten out of thirty Dow Jones companies have their headquarters in the sunny Cayman Islands, where all luxuries are available at their fingertips. In this way, many companies suck the blood out of the American tax system.[2] Even President Barack Obama expressed his amazement that twenty thousand American companies showed one address in the Cayman Islands as their registered company address. He said in one of his statements in May 2009 that either the building was the biggest building in the world, or it was the biggest scam in the world.[3] He contended that the American people knew exactly what it was. If so, then what immediate measures did the American government take to make the abusers of the system accountable for robbing state revenues? If the government or the president makes certain disclosures, reiterating what has already been known in financial circles for decades, then it is tantamount to merely appeasing public opinion.

Hedge funds, which are covered in detail later in this study, allow fund managers to "hedge their bets," to use the market expression, with the objective of controlling risk. They deal in derivatives and gain through price differentials or arbitrage. More

---

1 Mahmood Rafique, "Financial Frauds Cost Billions of Dollars in Losses: Poll," *Arab News*, October 23, 2008.

2 'Coke, Oracle, Intel use Cayman Islands to avoid US taxes', *Business Standard*, http://www.business-standard.com/article/companies/coke-oracle-intel-use-cayman-islands-to-avoid-us-taxes-109050600023_1.html, May 6, 2009.

3 'The building in tax haven that 20,000 firms call home: Cayman Islands has more companies than inhabitants', *Mail Online*, http://www.dailymail.co.uk/news/article-3411183/The-building-tax-haven-20-000-firms-call-home-Cayman-Islands-companies-registered-inhabitants.html, January 22, 2016.

than six thousand hedge funds owned by wealthy American individuals are in the Caribbean islands, away from the watchful eyes of the US Federal Reserve System.

It was an open secret for decades that offshore centers with lax legislation provided a safe haven for crime money. They also acted as fortresses for the wealth looted by despots, dictators, and tyrants from the public treasuries of their respective nations. Yet hardly anybody talked about introducing tighter controls and punishing the criminals. But when shadowy offshore banking systems started ripping off industrial nations, lamentation was heard at the G-20 summits that tighter controls needed to be introduced, that offshore safe havens needed to be regulated, and that the shadowy banking system needed to be scrapped. As long as the abusers were targeting uninformed investors and nations of the developing world, it was convenient for developed nations to turn a blind eye. But when they themselves became victims, they started talking in G-20 summits about introducing regulations in the interest of globalization. In this study, the role of offshore centers is investigated further.

According to the KPMG consultancy group's survey, more than £1 billion worth of fraud cases were heard by the UK courts in 2008. This was the second-highest record of fraud cases in the twenty-one-year history of the survey carried out by the firm. Mortgage fraud cases were valued at £36 million in 2008, ten times higher than in 2007. This figure multiplied as the effects of the credit crunch emerged gradually.

The Spanish police announced on January 28, 2009, that fraud worth $600 million involving the LSE was uncovered, followed by the arrest of six suspects. The fraud had begun in 2003, and it took more than five years for authorities to take action. This may well be just scratching the surface. There are likely to be thousands of cases the authorities or the watchdog organizations may never have time to look into because they are either understaffed, overworked, underfinanced, or demoralized. Hence, it has become a lucrative business for fraudsters to wind down in one financial center and get established under a different name in another center. In this way, they play a cat-and-mouse game with the authorities.

This study analyzes the types of games played in the stock market and exposes the extent to which the entire system is subjected to abuses. Nowadays, key financial and economic theories are thrown out of the window as invalid, which will be substantiated in this study through expert opinions. The stock market fluctuates on the basis of rumors and the flimsiest of reasons. For instance, if the governor of the Bank of England issues a statement that the economy will take some time to recover, share prices may start falling across the board. If the next day, a banker or financial expert issues a statement to the media that the worst part of the recession is over, the mood in the market may reverse. If Lehman Brothers in America declares its insolvency, this news may pull down all banking shares. The next day, if Chase Bank declares that its quarterly profits are better than expected, banking shares may reverse their trend. The unemployment figures published for the previous quarter may show that the number of people out of work is higher than expected. This may push the market south. The next day, the retail price index may be low, indicating that inflation is not as bad as had been forecast. This may push the market north. It all depends on expectations and forecasts that are hardly ever right.

In his book *The Crash of 2008 and What It Means*, George Soros eulogizes the demise of Lehman Brothers and laments the fact that US authorities allowed the firm to go bankrupt without coming to its rescue. But there is no meaningful condemnation of the bosses of Lehman Brothers for having taken irresponsible and unsustainable risks in its dealings and effectively mismanaging the funds investors entrusted to its representatives, as if this were their prerogative. At least, it seems that Soros speaks on behalf of many, if not most, observers when he asserts that the financial crisis, at the time of writing, was the worst since the 1930s. That view totally falsifies the theory that financial markets tend toward equilibrium or stability.[4] The similitude of the great economic crisis of 2007–8 was like "a once-in-a-century credit tsunami," in the words of former Federal Reserve Board chairman Alan Greenspan.[5]

The market players, including the authorities, cannot possibly muster perfect knowledge. Therefore, all the talk about the perfect market and the optimum price level is simply incomprehensible. Soros believes that the bursting of the housing bubble in the United States, which triggered the global financial crisis, is not the whole story; it is only half the story. The credit crunch, led by the United States, erupted in August 2007. This started pulling down all the major economies of the world and their financial systems, unmasking the unreal, unsustainable, and conjectural theories and premises on which the global financial order is built. Though the housing boom in the United States was based on fictitious grounds, which the banks were completely

4 Soros, vii.

5 Foster and Magdoff, 11.

aware of, this did not stop them from lending $9 trillion between 1997 and 2006 as collateral to home equity.[6] The mortgage debt of American households in this period exceeded the total mortgage debt since the mortgage market began.[7]

The calamity facing the US economy was felt in the emergency measures taken by the state of California, where its governor, former Hollywood actor Arnold Schwarzenegger, announced that state offices would be closed for three days each month until June 2010 and that employees would not be paid wages for those days. This desperate measure was meant to address the state's budget deficit of $24.3 billion. The federal budget deficit surpassed $1 trillion for the first time.

In Great Britain, the Bank of England disclosed in the beginning of July 2009 that UK residents owed £233 billion on credit cards, overdrafts, and other loans. Because of residents' heavy indebtedness, rogue traders and exploiters in the financial industry took undue advantage of the ill-informed public. At long last, the government was contemplating the introduction of some legislative controls over credit card checks. The unemployment figure in the United Kingdom published in the same month was the highest it had been for ten years.

The mood of the market is as fallible as the mood of investors. The total imperfection of financial and economic theories is reflected in price movements, which can become very erratic. However, it is institutional investors, not small investors, who are at the helm of the world of finance. The game being played in the financial and stock markets is explored critically in this study to prove that far from being vehicles for economic development, they have caused disasters to the economy and to investors.

In June 2009, President Obama announced that he was introducing new regimes to regulate different areas of the financial industry. But almost simultaneously as the regulatory regimes were introduced, shadowy antisocial criminal elements emerged, flexing their own expertise to thwart any attempts by the authorities to regulate the industry. New measures were planned to evade the laws, whether they were tax legislation, reporting requirements, or any other controls.

The negative face of capitalism has manifested in recent years through corporate crimes and scandals that have rocked Western and Eastern capitalism. At one time, people thought that despotic and dictatorial systems bred corrupt politicians. The

6 Soros, xv.

7 Ibid., 85.

events and scandals in the democratic systems of the West involving democratically elected members of Parliament proved that the capitalist system itself is corrupt at the core. People have become accustomed to serving self-interest at the cost of public interest. The scandals that were unraveled in the English Parliament by the press and media in relation to expense claims by MPs and cabinet ministers showed that the system is so fragile that it can be manipulated by none other than lawmakers, who are supposed to set high moral standards of honesty. There are two causes of every political and financial crisis and behind every breach of trust and ethical values: selfish motives and greed. This study demonstrates, through real-life scenarios, how these factors have wrought disasters to people's livelihoods and destroyed economies.

A lot of technical terminology is used in the course of discussion and analysis. For that reason, a glossary of terms and their definitions that are relevant to this study appears at the end of this book for your convenience.

CHAPTER 1

BANKS LEAD THE WAY TO DECLINE

The Black Monday of October 6, 2008, saw the world's stock markets sink deep into murky waters. The London stock market recorded the largest one-day fall in twenty years. Household banks on both sides of the Atlantic started collapsing as the International Monetary Fund warned that the world financial system was facing a "systematic meltdown."[8] The financial analysts who were still adamant or overconfident in using illusionary phrases like "market adjustment" or "forces of supply and demand" were either trying to keep their businesses afloat by misleading the investors—or living in Alice's Wonderland. That fantasy novel might have been literary nonsense in its time, but a greater nonsense in our time is the financial and economic fantasy aimed at preying on innocent members of the public and misguiding them into believing that the financial and stock markets provide a reliable mechanism for capital growth.

Investors who are lured into the trap of parting with their money may never make it to the shore. Some may go on sinking deeper and deeper into muddy waters. Yet there are investors who are seduced to participate in this risky speculative game, with those who gain doing so at the expense of those who lose out. The ones who sustain losses are normally the misinformed, who act according to the conjecture and false representations by crooks among stockbrokers. It is not in the interest of these stockbrokers to give accurate information to would-be investors. They may feel very uneasy and awkward when asked to disclose all the information about the funds on their recommended list. At most, they may graciously refer investors to the barely readable

8 International Monetary Fund annual report 2009, https://www.imf.org/external/pubs/ft/ar/2009/eng/pdf/ar09_eng.pdf.
'The Financial and Economic crisis of 2008-2009 and developing countries', United Nations Conference on trade and development, http://unctad.org/en/Docs/gdsmdp20101_en.pdf, December 2010.

small print, which can be interpreted in different ways. In any case, they might not disclose the hefty commissions the funds may be paying them for promoting their dubious investment schemes. Even if there is an investment advisory agreement in force, they know for sure that very few investors bother to read the exception clauses in small print, framed in complicated and technical terms. But for the purpose of saving their skin from future litigation, this is called "compliance with the law."

The financial and economic meltdown compelled governments in the capitalist world to adopt interventionist measures. As much as the last century saw a spectacular collapse of the socialist and communist systems, the aging capitalist system seems to be sinking deep into the trap laid down by its greed. In a nutshell, unquenchable greed, covetousness, and exploitation of the vulnerable are the common factors that brought down socialism and communism and are also behind the aging capitalist system that is dragging on.

On October 8, 2008, the British government approved a package of half a trillion pounds to bail out ailing banking institutions that were being mismanaged by executives who earned salary packages, bonuses, and share-incentive schemes of millions of pounds. The victims, more often than not, turned out to be members of the public, small investors, pensioners, and endowment policyholders. Four days later, Robert Zoellick, the World Bank president, declared in a press conference that "this has been a manmade catastrophe."[9]

The October 2008 turbulence on the world's stock markets and the meltdown of the banking sector—the worst since the great stock market crash of 1987—made a mockery of the ideals of capitalism. Governments on both sides of the Atlantic deemed it pertinent to rescue the estranged banks before the meltdown afflicted the entire financial and economic world. Western governments injected billions of taxpayers' money to save banks that had ended up in a quagmire of overlending as a result of the negligent and imprudent policies of their highly paid executives. In developed and developing countries, which had been inundated with external debts, the stock market seemed to have become a mechanism for misallocation of wealth and resources. No new wealth was created, but wealth was maneuvered and manipulated to end up

9 "Financial crisis is 'man-made catastrophe'", says World Bank chief, *The Telegraph*, http://www.telegraph.co.uk/finance/financialcrisis/3187467/Financial-crisis-is-man-made-catastrophe-says-World-Bank-chief.html, October 13, 2008.

in the coffers of those who were proficient at playing the game at the expense of others who were not.

The British government adopted socialist measures by effectively nationalizing the troubled banks. Therefore, phrases like "reconstruction" and "readjustment" that financial analysts used in the aftermath of partial nationalization sounded shallow. The prime minister of the United Kingdom at the time, Gordon Brown, said in a press conference on October 13, 2008,[10] that because of "irresponsibility or excessive risk taking" by bank executives, "the rest of us have paid." As if excessive risk-taking and the ensuing results were not enough, but to add insult to injury, the bank executives voted for themselves phenomenal bonuses.[11]

This global financial crisis was not the first and certainly will not be the last. When a catastrophe occurs on such a mammoth scale, it adversely affects retailers, wholesalers, manufacturers, and consumers. With figures showing the worst decline of confidence in manufacturing in the past twenty-eight years, consumers were set to pay the price of the imminent recession lurking over their heads. Even the car industry in the United Kingdom had to be bailed out when the government announced that it was pumping in £2.3 billion to rescue the industry from heavily falling demand. The independent Institute for Fiscal Studies (IFS) reported that the UK government debt would last twenty years.

Following the announcement of the rescue plan by the government, the London stock market rebounded and started to rise after a weeklong heavy fall. The honeymoon lasted only two days as the gambling spree of speculators withered away. On October 15, 2008, when unemployment figures were announced, showing the biggest quarterly increase in seventeen years, the London stock market plunged sharply and wiped out all the preceding gains.

In the wake of the economic crisis that was triggered by the financial crisis, many people were flabbergasted at the sheer magnitude of the crisis and wondered what went so drastically wrong that the world of banking and finance fell not to its knees but on its face. This question would have been reasonable had everything been right

---

10 Pres conference, https://www.theguardian.com/business/2008/oct/13/marketturmoil-creditcrunch, October 13, 2008.

11 Sam Fleming, 'Greed that fuelled the crash: How city fat cats took home £17bn bonuses… as their banks crumbled', *Mail Online*, http://www.dailymail.co.uk/news/article-1077120/Greed-fuelled-crash-How-city-fat-cats-took-home-17bn-bonuses--banks-crumbled.html, October 14, 2008.

in the first place and things had started going wrong thereafter. But this was not so. Things were wrong at the roots, and they had never been right. The foundation of the financial world is built on sand, not on concrete. The underlying motive is to prey on the weak, the elderly, and young couples, to sell them financial products, including mortgages, at terms and conditions that are not in their best interest but in the best interest of the financial institutions.

Terms used in the gambling world like "spread betting," "flutter," "punter," "risk spreading," and so forth are also used in the stock market speculation game. In the gambling world and stock markets, there are winners and losers. Just as gamblers cannot rationalize their betting decisions but rather depend on abstract techniques of intuition and so-called luck, so do the players in the stock market. In the gambling world, the minority causes disasters to the interest of the majority of the members of the public, who are not involved in the gambling spree; the same scenario applies in stock markets too. Those who become rich through the stock market game are a tiny minority, but those who end up losing their capital are an overwhelming majority. The rich become richer because of misinformation and unawareness generated purposefully. Their interest is best served in keeping investors and pensioners blindfolded, or at best, half-informed.

The abuses of the system and corporate fraud have made headlines for decades and have not abated at all. The victims almost always are the vast majority of small investors who trust the system with their lifetime savings, pensions, and insurance funds. They take the financial institutions and stock markets at face value, believing that all the parties abide by the letter of the law. But this is clearly not true. Sometimes the law-enforcing authorities themselves remain baffled when their own supervision proves to be deficient and flawed, as has been well illustrated in the aftermath of some of the major collapses, like that of Bank of Credit and Commerce International (BCCI) in the early nineties of the last century and its meltdown and subsequent nationalization of the giant mortgage lender Northern Rock Building Society.

In contrast with BCCI, Northern Rock was a homebred financial institution, so it should have been supervised with diligence. Financial analysts disagree about the main cause for its humiliating plight. Some claim that it was because of overexposure to the failing US subprime-mortgage market, whereas others claim that it was the result of its executives' careless and negligent lending policies. Consequently, a bank run began the following day on Friday, with long queues outside its branches. News on September 17, 2007, stated that customers had withdrawn an estimated £2 billion of retail deposits within three days, since the bank had applied for emergency funds.

On March 11, 2008, another bank run began on Bear Stearns in the United States. Within two days, its capital base of $17 billion was reduced to $2 billion in cash.

This shows that what keeps banks and lending institutions buoyant is not the skyscrapers and lavishly furnished and decorated buildings that house them or the extravagance projected in their public relations but public confidence. As soon as the public smells a rat in their dealings and gets the offensive taste of their false and spurious claims, the credibility of these institutions gets badly battered. When this happens, the public can no longer be tricked into believing that the asset base of these institutions is strong enough to sustain the flood of cash withdrawals en masse. It is the public confidence that keeps them afloat, and it is the lack of public confidence that brings them to their knees. A trail of failures of giant financial institutions illustrates the artificial framework of the system, which operates on a trial-and-error basis. For instance, an ombudsman report released in July 2008 on the collapse of Equitable Life Insurance Company found a "decade of regulatory failure." As a result, more than one million insurance policyholders lost their savings.[12]

The failure of Landsbanki, Glitnir, Heritable and Kaupthing Singer and Friedlander, the collapsed banks in Iceland was a case in point of the unreliability of the financial system in the capitalist world. These banks housed migrated funds of a billion pounds of local councils in the United Kingdom.[13] By October 2008, when the banks were in deep trouble, they declared that they were freezing account holders' funds because of the run on their funds. But the British government promised to do everything it could to recover the local government funds, which had found a safe haven not in the domestic accounts but in Iceland. Iceland resorted to raising its interest rate to 18 percent to clear the menace of its own creation.

The crisis in the financial and housing markets had been triggered by the United States and was spreading like cancerous cells across Europe. The Bank of England estimated that the financial losses to financial companies arising from credit crises

12 'Justice delayed: The Ombudsman's House of Commons Public Administration Second Report on Equitable Life, http://www.publications.parliament.uk/pa/cm200809/cmselect/cmpubadm/41/41i.pdf, December 11, 2008.

13 PatrickWintour and Audrey Gillan. 'Lost in Iceland: £1 billion from councils, charities and police', *The Guardian*, https://www.theguardian.com/business/2008/oct/10/banking-iceland, October 10, 2008.

were expected to be £1.8 trillion ($2.8 trillion). It also estimated that 1.2 million homeowners were likely to end up with negative equity if house prices kept on falling at the same pace. In its financial-stability report, the Bank of England reported that £5 trillion of British taxpayers' money was allocated to save the giant banks in the British banking system. Amid a certainty of global financial collapse engineered by the banking world, Barclays bank announced a proposed scheme to raise £7.3 billion through the state and through private funds of the royal families of Middle Eastern countries, especially Qatar and Abu Dhabi, whose leaders were eager to rescue the failing banks.

In the United States, mortgage brokers and lenders joined hands to encourage the new scheme called NINJA loans (no income, no job, no assets) as borrowers produced false accounts at best and no accounts at worst. Soros paints a factual scenario of the predicament in which liabilities exceeded assets and there was no way to honor these collateralized debt obligations (CDOs) that were piling up against the same assets. The value of credit default swaps (CDSs) outstanding was $42.6 trillion, equivalent to total household income in the United States, whereas the stock market capitalization was $18.5 trillion. Soros states that Alan Greenspan simply turned a blind eye to the flagrant abuse reported in the subprime-mortgage schemes. He explains how homeowners' equity was being wiped out as mortgage hedge funds fell, one after another.[14]

Robert Pollin, a professor of economics and codirector of the Political Economy Research Institute at the University of Massachusetts Amber, writes, "The financial crisis of 2007–08 and with more certainty in store for 2009 and beyond, is one of the great calamities of modern neoliberal capitalism."[15]

This was happening under the very nose of Congress (the legislature), the Securities and Exchange Commission, and world-renowned professors of economics whom Harvard or any other American university would take pride in producing. They were acting as if they did not know what type of economic and financial catastrophe was in the offing.

Mervyn King, the governor of the Bank of England, told BBC on November 12, 2008, that this was the biggest banking crisis since the First World War. He said that

14 Soros, xix–xx.

15 Foster and Magdoff, 2.

"these are difficult and unprecedented times."[16] Indeed, after every financial collapse and stock market bust, officials are quick to lament that these are exceptional times. The fact that the menace repeats itself each decade should have made investors realize that the system itself is so fragile that the exception is becoming the rule. When the economy takes a downward turn because of elites' negligence, the middle and lower classes are expected to make sacrifices and pay the price. Rarely is any voice raised to make the fat cats, who have milked millions out of the economy, pay the price for their mismanagement. Later, a committee of MPs warned that the bankers had made an "astonishing mess," the effects of which would be felt for generations to come.[17] The Treasury Committee of the UK Parliament reported that the crisis had been caused by banks' reckless behavior.

Sir John Gieve, the deputy governor of the Bank of England, confessed in an interview on BBC Panorama on December 21, 2008, that the bank did not understand the severity of economic problems. It had known that "crazy borrowing" was taking place and that the prices of houses and other assets were rising without sustainability. Apparently, the bank relied only on the interest rate to control the economy. The bank's leadership should have known the basic economic principle that whatever rises dramatically without the support of economic fundamentals has to fall dramatically too. The Governor of the Bank of England further said: "Since mid-September, the global banking system has experienced its most serious disruption for almost a century.[18] Later on, the House of Lords Economic Affairs Committee severely criticized the so-called tripartite system, through which the Treasury, the Bank of England, and the Financial Services Authority were supposed to be supervising the banking system. But the committee said the tripartite system was a failure, turning the banking regulation into a failure too.

Guardian research showed that leading European banks set aside £7.45 billion to cover six-month staff costs, including discretionary bonuses for seventy-two thousand investment bankers.[19] The Royal Bank of Scotland announced the loss

---

16 Bank of England statement in full, *The Telegraph*, http://www.telegraph.co.uk/finance/personalfinance/interest-rates/3391011/Bank-of-England-statement-in-full.html, November 6, 2008.

17 "Banks 'author of their own demise' ", politics.co.uk, http://www.politics.co.uk/news/2009/5/1/banks-authors-of-their-own-demise May 1, 2009.

18 Bank of England statement in full, op. cit.

19 'State-supported investment banks set billions aside for bonuses', *Guardian*, https://www.theguardian.com/business/2008/nov/03/european-bank-bonuses-executive-salaries, November 3, 2008.

of £24.1 billion in 2008, the biggest in UK corporate history. It had to be bailed out with £20 billion of taxpayers' money. It set aside £1.7 billion for staff compensation. Its finance director, Guy Whittaker, was paid £829,000. He was sadly deprived of a bonus and special pension, although he graciously waived a long-term share option.

The last member of Sir Fred Goodwin's top management at the Royal Bank of Scotland was to retire with £517,000-a-year pension. The deputy chief executive, Gordon Pell, retired with a pension of £9.8 million.[20]

Barely two months of this catastrophe had passed when on January 4, 2009, business secretary Lord Mandelson had to issue a word of warning to the executive of the Royal Bank of Scotland (RBS). This warning followed a report in *The Times* (UK) that the bank planned to award large bonuses, despite the expectation of huge losses in its financial statements and despite the fact that its shares prices were reduced to a few pennies. The business secretary issued a word of caution that if the bank voted "exorbitant" bonuses for its bosses, it took the risk of alienating itself in public opinion.

As part of the deal to save RBS from disgrace, its chief executive, Stephen Hester, agreed not to redeem shares worth £3.4 million until 2014. It was expected at the time that this generous gesture on the part of the boss of RBS would work out for the benefit of the bank because it would not have to cough up such a large amount immediately. By 2014, RBS shares were most likely to recover from the shock of reaching the verge of total collapse. The chief executive's holding represented a share-option scheme as part of a new pay package potentially worth £9.6 million.[21]

But the modern-day reality of the corporate world indicates that the interest of shareholders or investors is the first to be sacrificed in times of crisis. In many cases, the directors are employees of the companies. Therefore, their multimillion-dollar packages are guaranteed and are covered as fixed expenditures against profits in the

20 'Pell quits RBS with £9.8m pension', *Financial Times*, http://www.ft.com/cms/s/0/24737b06-3a9f-11de-8a2d-00144feabdc0.html#axzz4FQ1nHvlz, May 7, 2009.

21 'RBS chief Stephen Hester set for £ 9.6m incentive package', *Independent*, http://www.independent.co.uk/news/business/news/rbs-chief-stephen-hester-set-for-pound96m-incentive-package-1712427.html, June 22, 2009.

'Former RBS boss Stephen Hester set for £500,000 payout from bailed-out bank - more than two years after he left', *Financial Mail on Sunday*, http://www.thisismoney.co.uk/money/news/article-3435249/Former-Royal-Bank-Scotland-boss-Stephen-Hester-course-final-payout-bailed-organisation-500000-two-years-left.html#ixzz4EhCFJU00, February 6, 2016.

financial statements. In their capacity as shareholders, they may or may not hold a controlling interest in the company. Either way, they are better off getting a fixed-salary package that is guaranteed whether the company makes a profit or suffers a loss. In this case too, outside investors or shareholders end up losing not only profit but also capital value of their shares if the company continues posting losses.

Many companies make a provision in their memorandums of association that the company has a right to buy back its own ordinary share capital. What guarantee is there that the directors, mustering a controlling interest in the company, are not the ones playing roulette with their active participation in the speculative game in the shares of their own company to give the impression to outside investors that there is upward activity? Once they are able to attract enough money from outside investors, the share prices might cease to rise. As the speculative game played by the directors ends, share prices might start to fall sharply, to the detriment of outside investors who have been lured into thinking that it was worthwhile to invest in the company, which showed an upward trend in its share price. Psychologically, shareholders are averse to taking losses. As a result, they might wait in vain, pinning their hopes on the possibility that share prices will rise again. This is how outside investors, unaware of insider dealings, may be deceived.

Critics say that if there is any sense of fairness in the capitalist corporate world, then directors' pay should be directly related to performance figures. If executives persistently fail to deliver or their policies contribute to the downfall of their companies, then they should be deprived of their multimillion-dollar pay packages. Executive pay in the modern corporate world is one of the contentious areas that need strict governmental control if any credibility is to be attached to the estranged financial system.

As the tragic events of the financial world unfolded, the Bank of England announced on November 6, 2008, that it was cutting the bank's base rate by 1.5 percent, to 3 percent. The media described this remedy as "shock therapy."[22] The last time the rate was as low as 3 percent was in 1955. On December 4, 2008, the bank cut the base rate again by 1 percent, to 2 percent, a fifty-seven-year low. If anything, such a reaction reflected a desperate attempt at saving the strangled economy from a serious slump. But many analysts noted that the banks were determined to pursue their

22 Ashley Seager et al., 'Shock as Bank of England slashes rate to 3%, *The Guardian*, https://www.theguardian.com/business/2008/nov/06/interestrates-interestrates2, November 6, 2008.

extortion policy by being reluctant to pass the reduction in the cost of borrowing to consumers.

There was a 220 percent increase in companies becoming insolvent (bankrupt) in England and Wales in the last quarter of 2008, compared to the same period in 2007. It should have come as no surprise that every five minutes, somebody was going bankrupt in the United Kingdom.[23] When inflation rises, the consumer is crushed under the rising prices. When a recession besets the economy and unemployment rises in the wake of falling demand, the consumer takes the beating. Whether the cost of borrowing rises or falls, the helpless consumer gets exploited in the debt-ridden economy. Even as the bank rate was being slashed, credit card companies were increasing their rates and ripping off consumers through exorbitant service charges. In an exploitative economy, the prime aim is to promote consumerism even, through manipulative advertisements. When naïve members of the public get stuck in debt, the interest of credit card companies is protected and takes precedence over the interest of borrowers.

One would expect that the reduction of the bank rate would have helped the high street banks and consumers buy more and would have stimulated demand during the shopping craze of the season in light of the approaching Christmas period. But this did not work as expected. So the Bank of England took another radical step on February 5, 2009, by reducing the bank rate to 1 percent—the lowest in its 315-year history—to stimulate the badly battered economy. Even this measure did not work. So the bank took another drastic step, lowering the rate by 0.5 percent, to 0.5 percent, on March 5, 2009—the lowest ever. This means the bank rate was slashed from 5 percent in August 2008 to 0.5 percent in March 2009. Since October 2008, the interest rate had been reduced six times. Rather than print more banknotes, this measure taken by the bank, called "quantitative easing," was expected to pump £75 billion into the economy to enable commercial banks to lend more to their customers.

The scenario on the other side of the Atlantic was no less frantic. Bank of America, the largest and one of the strongest US banks, was salvaged from the wreckage with $20 billion in government aid and $118 billion in guarantees against bad assets (meaning irrecoverable debts). Much of its loss emanated from its bad decision to buy

23 "Credit Crash Britain Money for Nothing," BBC money program, BBC 2, http://www.bbc.co.uk/programmes/b00fcvrl, November 6, 2008.

Merrill Lynch. This bailout was in addition to the $25 billion the bank received from the Troubled Asset Relief Program (TARP). Merrill Lynch posted a $15.3 billion loss for the fourth quarter of 2008, while Bank of America reported a $1.7 billion loss for the same period.[24] The US Senate approved additional funding of $250 billion to TARP.

On the other side of the vicious spectrum, Citigroup reported a loss of $8.29 billion, despite being rescued a few months earlier with $45 billion and $306 billion in guarantees by the US government. Ben Bernanke, the US Federal Reserve chairman, confessed that this was the worst financial crisis since the 1930s. The new Obama administration compromised, funneling $787 billion into the economy.

As the agonizing tale of the ailing financial world unfolded, British Petroleum (BP) reported that its quarterly profits from July to September 2008 had more than doubled to 148 percent from the previous year due to an exorbitant rise in oil prices. The oil prices, which had risen to a record level of $147 a barrel, had adversely affected every household. Despite the fact that this was putting enormous pressure on the living budget of the middle and lower classes, the elite class was reaping the benefits. Profits from the limited resources of the lower class in society were ending up in the coffers of the capitalists. Due to increases in oil prices, Royal Dutch Shell reported a profit of $4.8 billion in the fourth quarter of 2008, compared to a profit of $6.7 billion in the same period in 2007, but its annual profit for 2008 rose by 14 percent, to $31.4 billion—one of the highest in corporate history in the United Kingdom or Europe. Although oil prices witnessed a drastic decline after that, the contrast of imbalance or maladjustment of resources in the economy was too obvious to conceal. Under both contrasting scenarios, the middle and lower classes were being trampled.

The collapse of public companies and financial institutions does not emerge overnight. The factors leading to collapse build up over a period of time. Small investors who buy and sell shares are simply not in a position to know the intricacies and complexities that govern the stock market mechanism and performance. There are certain economic factors that directly affect the market, like the rate of inflation or deflation, growth or recession, unemployment figures, wholesale and retail price indices, and the interest rate, which are the bread and butter of the capitalist economy. However, certain internal factors also play havoc with the prices of shares, like misrepresentation

24 'Bank of America bail-out agreed', BBC News, http://news.bbc.co.uk/1/hi/business/7832484.stm, January 16, 2009.

of facts, sensational reports in the press, exaggerated performance data, insider dealings, speculation, and widespread fraud.

American investor Warren Buffett told an interesting story in his annual letter to the shareholders of Berkshire Hathaway Inc. in 1985,[25] warning that financial institutions, with their highly paid executives and a troop of staff members, could not possibly bar instability. According to the story, Saint Peter was said to stop an oil prospector from entering his heavenly abode, to which the protestor protested strongly. He was told that Saint Peter would have liked to let him in, but the place was congested with oilmen. The oil prospector sought permission from Saint Peter to say just five words, which he was granted. So he shouted, "Oil is discovered in hell!" As soon as his voice echoed, all the oilmen rushed out of the heavenly abode to enter hell. Once the place was empty, Saint Peter told the oil prospector that he could now enter heaven in peace. But the prospector refused, saying that he would rather accompany the rest of the oilmen; after all, there must be some truth in the rumor!

This is precisely what happened in the bust of 2008 in the financial and stock markets. The financiers and market makers marched ceremoniously toward a hell of their own making.

There have been cases in which even the audited statutory accounts published and filed by companies or corporations have proved to be false. The dividends that companies declare can be misleading. There have been instances in which unscrupulous directors of offshore companies have taken undue advantage of lax rules and regulations by declaring dividends from shareholders' equity via share-capital accounts and share-premium accounts. This means that a company might be posting losses yet go on paying an attractive rate of dividend to give a false impression to shareholders that it is a profit-making company. The extra money the shareholders pay initially at the time of the issue of shares, over and above their nominal value, is then misused to conceal the true financial position of the company until the value of the company's shares tumbles dramatically.

Many such fraudulent dealings are spread across the financial world. But one case of a stockbroker in America that attracted a media furor is the best example to illustrate this point. It has to be noted that this fraud continued for a long time in a well-regulated financial center without raising regulators' suspicion.

---

25 Golding, 162.

On December 13, 2008, international media reported the arrest of Bernard Madoff, a New York stockbroker, on charges of swindling his clients by as much as $65 billion. The swindle was classified as the biggest embezzlement of funds committed by a sole stockbroker. The fraudulent dealings were disguised as hedged funds that paid investors very attractive dividends from profits that did not exist at all. In the aftermath of his arrest, his defense lawyer issued a statement saying, "Bernard Madoff is a longstanding leader in the financial services industry...He is a person of integrity."[26] An ex-chairman of the NASDAQ stock market, he would have been ranked in the aristocratic class among the "right-thinking" members of society. Some reputable investment-fund managers and bankers trusted him blindly and dumped their clients' money into his hedged funds. This was gross negligence in handling clients' money.

Fund managers' pay is not performance related. They get paid even if they do not have to make decisions to buy and sell stocks but rather sit on their existing portfolios. Warren Buffett once exclaimed that he makes "more money when snoring than when active!"[27] In the late nineties, the top job at UK Public Limited companies during the bull market could have fetched around £3 million on success and £400,000 on failure.[28] This explains why, on the sudden turn of the market, some fund managers suffered from immobility, as if there were shackles around their necks.

The UK's UniCredit SpA's Pioneer Alternative Investments put "substantially all" of its almost $280 million Primeo Select Fund with Madoff, according to a fact sheet on Pioneer's website. The casualties of this swindle were some of the big names in the European banking system, including Britain's HSBC; the Royal Bank of Scotland; Spain's largest bank, Santander, which owns the UK's high street banks Abbey, Alliance & Leicester and Bradford & Bingley; Japan's Nomura; and France's Natixis and BNP Paribas, with the aggregate potential losses running into billions of dollars.[29]

---

26 'Market maker Bernard L. Madoff arrested in $50B 'giant Ponzi scheme', *Wiki News, https://en.wikinews.org/wiki/Market_maker_Bernard_L._Madoff_arrested_in_$50B_%27giant_Ponzi_scheme%27,* December 12, 2008.

27 Patrick Morris, 'Warren Buffett Tells You the Difference Between Stock Trading and Investing', *The Motley Fool*, http://www.fool.com/investing/general/2014/12/14/warren-buffett-tells-you-the-difference-between-st.aspx, December 14, 2014.

28 Golding, 171, 183.

29 Jon Menon and Charles Penty, "Madoff's 'Lie' Ensnares Victims From Paris to Tokyo", Bloomberg, http://www.canadianhedgewatch.com/content/news/general/?id=3875, December 15, 2008.

Like the fraudster Robert Maxwell, who did not spare even his own employees from the great fiddle of the twentieth century he masterminded, Madoff was ruthless in his dealings. It was claimed that he ripped off his own fellow billionaires—members of the rich men's synagogue, the place of worship of the Jewish faith in New York City. Madoff's scandal nullified the myth of efficiency and expertise of financial watchdog agencies like the Securities and Exchange Commission. Certain questions were bound to be asked during the course of investigation into the Madoff scandal: How did the auditors pass the accounts and issue clean audit reports? How can any responsible outside fund manager live in dreams to the extent of trusting a stockbroker running a one-man show? Why did the banks keep on lending without ensuring whether proper internal controls and internal checks were in force, when the fraudster, in his own words, was reaping the fruits of "one big lie"? But if the system tolerates a billion small lies under the slogan that everything is permissible in love, war, and business, then one big lie could cost the system billions of dollars in one stroke.

As the Associated Press reported on December 17, 2008, Madoff once advised the US government on ways to protect investors from scam artists when his own fraud was at an advanced stage. This was meant to divert attention away from his wrong-doing. Perhaps he counted on men of influence in the US Congress and Senate, who stood by him because of his so-called philanthropy and political donations. People like Madoff are motivated to carry out their looting with such confidence that nobody will put them on death row, and they end up with some ridiculous prison sentence like 150 years, which is more of a joke than a punishment. He appeared in court on March 10, 2009, and his attorney declared that he planned to plead guilty to eleven charges of fraud. Fox News reported on March 2, 2009, that Madoff claimed that he was entitled to keep a $7 million Manhattan apartment and $62 million in assets. It had earlier reported, on January 9, 2009, that he was about to send checks worth $173 million to family and friends just before his arrest.

Fox News further quoted real examples of Madoff's clients who ended up with profits greater than the principal amounts they invested initially. Having withdrawn in cash the net profits, not realized profits, but profits shown on paper, they were in a situation of claiming the unwithdrawn amounts, which comprised fictitious gains over and above the amounts invested. Madoff's website boasted, "Clients know that Bernard Madoff has a personal interest in maintaining an unblemished record of value, fair dealing, and high ethical standards that have always been the firm's hallmark." The problem with dishonest and untrustworthy stockbrokers is that when, under whatever false pretenses, they succeed in attracting funds from investors, they consider that they have either won a lottery or that they have inherited these funds from their granddads and are thus free to launder them at their will, rather than invest them in all honesty in the best interest of investors.

Nicola Horlick, the boss of the UK-based Bramdean Investments, told the BBC on December 15, 2008, "I think now it is very difficult for people to invest in things that are meant to be regulated in America because they have fallen down on the job."[30] If convicted, Madoff, age seventy, was likely to face a long prison sentence and $5 million in fines. In all probability, he would have been released from prison on account of ill health or good behavior, and his style would then have been a source of inspiration for other fraudsters to emulate. After all, his Ponzi scheme had been named after Charles Ponzi, who "notoriously used the technique in the United States as long back as 1903," as reported in BBC News on December 15, 2008. In a Ponzi scheme, an investment manager makes false claims of high returns to savers, unsubstantiated by any evidence of revenues or earnings, and misuses the funds new investors put in to repay the old investors.

The first casualty of the Madoff affair was an incident of suicide, reported on Christmas Eve. Thierry de la Villehuchet, a French fund manager who lived in extravagance but lost $1.4 billion of his clients' money, took his own life in his New York apartment. His clients were mostly French aristocrats. At least they benefited from his extravagant entertainment parties and were impressed by his hospitality.

On June 29, 2009, Madoff was sentenced to 150 years in prison. It was more a distasteful joke than punishment. One aggrieved investor said outside the Lower Manhattan court, "I hope his prison cell becomes his coffin." Another investor whose life Madoff had ruined said, "Let him burn in the depths of hell." Investors questioned what good his apology was after the pain he had caused to thousands of people[31]. Of course nothing could compensate for the worries, agony, and disasters to inves-

---

30 Jeffrey Stinson, 'Victims of Madoff's alleged Wall Street scam spread to Europe', *USA Today*, http://abcnews.go.com/Business/story?id=6467617&page=1, n.d.

31 'Victims react to Madoff's sentencing', *Wall Street Journal video*, http://www.wsj.com/video/victims-react-to-madoff-sentencing/541815EA-1FB9-4F05-B620-6ABFFB267029.html, June 29, 2009.

tors and their families that would last much longer than his own life on this earth. His fraud, categorized as the worst in history and perpetrated for decades under the watchful eyes of regulators, successfully robbed investors of $50 billion to $65 billion. The question that remains is, if US authorities have been able to recover only £1 billion (at the time of writing), why is nobody advocating that regulators must investigate the group or nation that directly benefited from the disappearance of irrecoverable billions? Somebody must have assisted with laundering the funds.

Manipulative capitalism has acquired a status of a monstrous idol that is worshipped in the psyche of greedy materialists. Consequently, the system has become a breeding ground for many other Madoffs who are yet in the pipelines. One of them emerged on the surface in the post-Madoff saga. As reported by BBC News on June 19, 2009, the US Justice Department charged Texan billionaire Sir Allen Stanford with a $7 billion scheme to defraud investors. Sir Allen was already facing civil suits of $8 billion for allegedly defrauding investors. His Stanford International Bank, which issued phony certificates of deposit (CDs), was based in Antigua. If convicted, he could face a prison sentence of 250 years simply because he did not plead guilty as Madoff did. Some observers questioned these phony prison sentences for phony schemes. A White House spokesman did confess that "the outsized greed" of some robbed millions of people of their savings.

The BBC report also disclosed that Sir Allen had allegedly made "corrupt payments" to the former head of Antigua's financial services regulatory commission. It is noteworthy that this is the type of person who is responsible for protecting laws and regulations in the phony financial centers of West Indies. What is being uncovered may be only the tip of the iceberg. There must be many more Ponzi schemes loitering around the world.

Sir Allen is 205th on the list of America's richest tycoons, with his personal wealth estimated at $2.2 billion. In Antigua and Barbados, he is the largest private employer. After a $20 million cricket match he hosted between West Indies and English cricket players in 2008, he had to apologize to the English players for being too friendly with their wives and girlfriends.[32]

---

32 "Stanfold Charged with Fraud in US," BBC News, http://news.bbc.co.uk/1/hi/world/americas/8109690.stm. June 19, 2009.

Secret documents seen by the BBC Panorama team showed that both the US and British governments knew since 1990 that Sir Allen's investment funds had embezzled investors' money, and he was suspected of alleged money laundering. Yet nothing was done to come to the rescue of twenty-eight thousand depositors. In 1999, both the governments knew about a check of $3.1 million that he had paid by way of donation to the Drug Enforcement Administration.[33]

If financial statements are concocted, then it becomes difficult for regulatory regimes, even if they are vigilant, to trace the embezzlement of funds committed by reputable companies, much less the phony and Ponzi funds and their managers.

Many investors have a mistaken belief that if a company has a strong fixed-asset base, it is financially sound. Nothing could be further from the truth. These companies take secured and unsecured loans against their fixed assets to the extent that if they are liquidated, shareholders may not get any compensation for their shares, which have become valueless. Even companies that were once part of the FTSE 100 have simply disappeared. Prior to the meltdown of the dotcom and telecom shares, some giant companies lost more than 90 percent of their share values. Ten years after that, these companies had badly failed to regain even 20 percent of the lost values of their shares.

The losses eat away capital as termites eat away wood. This nullifies the erroneous notion that investment in shares and stocks is a long-term venture. The market is totally unreliable for small investors in the short term as well as the long term. By studying the accounts of certain telecom companies and analyzing their performance figures, one cannot fail to notice that as the shareholders of these companies were losing capital value of their shares persistently over the course of a decade, employee costs, including executives' salaries and bonuses, were rising.

In his work, Golding quotes certain practical examples to show that in any one day, the number of shares traded on the market is far less than the net worth of a company. A mining company called Rio Tinto, worth around £14 billion (at the time of writing), traded around four million shares worth around £50 million. A company worth £100 million would find it difficult to trade on all days. In November 2001, although the British Airways share price soared by 17 percent in a day in the wake of a drop in oil prices, fewer than 2 percent of its shares were traded.[34]

33 Panorama: "The Six Billion Dollar Man," BBC 1, May 11, 2009.

34 Golding, 71–72.

In the corporate world, abuse can take many forms. The dotcom and telecom bust succeeded in wiping out more than 90 percent of the value of shares within a couple of years. This did not stop executives from resorting to another extortion policy as a face-saving device. The directors, having a controlling interest in the companies, passed resolutions for capital reconstruction, such as the exchange of one new share for every ten thousand old shares held. Such a resolution acted as a double-edged sword for wiping out the holdings of outside or minority shareholders and artificially boosting share prices of the remnant from a few pennies to a couple of pounds. To a naïve and uninformed investor, a sudden boost in the share price of the reconstructed company, as quoted in the financial press, would give the impression that there was a dramatic improvement in performance, which was not the case at all. The technique may have succeeded in preying on uninformed investors and misleading them in committing their funds to mismanaged companies.

As the recession deepened from the first six months of 2009 onward, the mismanaged corporations queued up to declare insolvency. By the beginning of June 2009, General Motors, a car manufacturer that was the symbol of the American corporate world, was due to declare bankruptcy. This was to be the biggest case of manufacturing bankruptcy in American corporate history, with the controlling interest of General Motors (nicknamed Government Motors) to be passed to the US government.

The institution and functionality of the stock market carries different perceptions for different classes of people and organizations. Not all the people who deal on the market understand the rules and regulations that govern the intricacies of this market. Small investors and laymen might not fully comprehend the role the stock market plays in raising equity and loan capital and the underlying regulatory regime for floating shares of a public company. Indeed, many investors, especially those with surplus cash and savings, may enter the market to make a quick gain or a quick kill and get out as quickly as they went in. Yet many of them get stuck with unanticipated losses and declining share prices. If they are not careful and diligent before entering the market, it may take them some time to assimilate the rules of the game.

Many small investors, especially newcomers to the market who make impulsive rather than rational investment decisions, are not aware that the world's stock markets crash with a cyclical occurrence. When a crash occurs, the first casualties are not the giant institutional investors or stock dealers but small investors. Even the best expertise cannot predict a sudden bust in the market, although the symptoms may have been apparent but remained unheeded.

According to figures issued by the International Monetary Fund, funds managed by institutional investors between 1990 and 1998 more than doubled, to more than $30 trillion.[35]

There are individuals who have made money by playing the game the right way from their own perspectives, which may not apply to small investors. The strategy of these affluent and institutional investors is governed by very complex models, formulas, and expertise, which at times experts and top executives themselves do not fully understand. When such a risky strategy backfires, it wipes out gains from managed funds, pension funds, insurance funds, and savings, as has transpired in the aftermath of all the major crashes of the stock market, when pensioners end up being robbed in broad daylight. On April 20, 2009, BBC News reported, "The recession is putting pension schemes at greater risk of fraud, dishonesty, or risky behavior by employers," quoting the pension regulator.[36] This of course requires that scheme trustees, advisors, members, and auditors remain alert, lest the likes of Robert Maxwell help themselves to the pension funds of their employees.

In 1963, individuals owned 54 percent of shares by values; in 1981, they owned 28 percent, and in 2000 only 16 percent. The trend was increasingly shifting toward institutional investors. Large and medium-sized British companies may have had as much as an 80 to 90 percent stake of institutional investors, compared to 60 to 65 percent in the United States. The 1995 Pensions Act was a reaction to the ease with which the fraudster Maxwell was able to manipulate the pension funds of his employees.[37]

---

35 Golding, 101.

36 'Pension regulator warns on fraud', BBC-news, http://news.bbc.co.uk/1/hi/business/8007674.stm, April 20. 2009.

37 Golding, 22–24, 106.

CHAPTER 2

THE ROLE OF THE STOCK MARKET IN THE MARKET ECONOMY

This chapter focuses on the factors that lead to boom-and-bust in the stock market, which is the market in which securities—stocks, shares, fixed-interest bonds, and so on—are bought and sold. It is also called the "equity market."

Some companies quoted on the stock market display clear warnings to potential shareholders before they buy shares, such as the following:

1. The price and value of any investments and income therefrom, if any, can fluctuate and may fall against the investor's interest.
2. You may not get the original amount invested.
3. You should not invest an amount you cannot afford to lose.
4. Information on past performance is not a guide to future performance.
5. Changes in rates of exchange may have an adverse effect on the value of investments that have an exposure to foreign currencies.

Not all investors read the small print. The vast majority blindly rely on the recommendations of their stockbrokers.

There are unscrupulous dealers who do not give any warnings of risk to their clients, who may have relied on their judgment. The motive of such dealers is to maximize their brokerage without working in the best interest of their clients, particularly if they are able to exploit investors' gullibility. At times, these types of dealers act on behalf of companies that may be facing financial difficulties and looking for uninformed investors who do not make the slightest effort to probe their past-performance records and financial statements. To rely too much on stockbrokers or dealers and not to question their intentions may result in the victimization of small investors.

The concept of the stock market and its development was the brainchild of capitalist and pseudo-capitalist economies. Western governments borrow trillions in their respective currencies every year, enough to cover several times the current and capital budgets of a number of Asian and African countries. Capital investment per head of the population in Asian and African countries, with the notable exception of Japan, is low compared to similar investments in European countries and North American states. Through a number of regulatory and tax regimes, governments of the developed world compete with each other to attract overseas investments to fulfill their borrowing requirements for capital projects. The stock market is the main vehicle for raising capital for the public and private sectors.

Exchange of goods and services, supported by bourse—money exchange—is as old as civilization. In developed economies, financial services are a major component of the service industry, which comprises shipping, banking, tourism, insurance, pension funds, professional services, and investment in stocks and shares. "Stocks" and "shares" are interchangeable terms. Stocks in the United States are what ordinary shares are in the United Kingdom. Financial services contribute substantial revenues to the national budget of developed countries. Therefore, these countries take meticulous care to formulate a legislative and regulatory framework under which the financial industry operates. Development of rules, regulations, and codes of conduct and discipline, supported by statute law and surveillance by watchdog organizations and regulators, is meant to add credibility to the financial services industry and attract international investors.

The activities of the stock market commenced in Amsterdam in the 1600s.[38] In a modern sense, this was the first financial market.[39] In terms of market capitalization of the quoted securities, the largest stock exchange—the building or institution where shares and stocks are bought and sold—is in New York,[40] followed by London[41] and Tokyo.[42] Through the mechanism of the stock market, which is at the hub of the financial industry, the government raises capital for public sector investment and economic development, and the private sector raises capital for business, manufacturing, and

38 *NBK*, 455. The Amsterdam Stock Exchange was established in 1611.

39 Morris, 4.

40 *NBK*, 456. The New York Stock Exchange was established in 1792.

41 Ibid., 455. The London Stock Exchange was founded in 1773.

42 www.tse.or.jp/english/about/history.html. The Tokyo Stock Exchange was founded in 1878.

industrialization. Capital needed for conducting research may fall under the ambit of both the public and private sectors. Capital is injected into the economy for economic progress, to build infrastructure for public utility projects, such as sanitation; clean and hygienic drinking water; agricultural and irrigation systems; and construction of dams, roads, schools, educational institutions, hospitals, and national health services. Long-term investments are also made in scientific and technological research, defense equipment, heavy machinery, ships, aircraft, power plants, nuclear reactors, and so forth. Governments borrow to finance their capital budgets and development plans. They issue fixed-interest securities, which are called "stocks" in the United Kingdom and "bonds" in the United States. In the United Kingdom, the government borrows by issuing gilt-edged securities, which have comparatively low fixed-interest rates but offer guaranteed repayment.

There have been several changes in the functioning of the stock market. Since 1997, FTSE 100 shares have been traded on the Stock Exchange Electronic Trading System (SETS). The *Financial Times* Stock Exchange index of the one hundred largest companies in the United Kingdom is also called FTSE, pronounced "footsie." Under this system, brokers advertise on behalf of their clients, who buy or sell large blocks of shares, stating the price range at which they would be prepared to deal. This facility is available to members of the LSE.

In the past, brokers would deal with the public, and jobbers would deal with the brokers. A jobber's commission was the difference between the buying price and the selling price. Like stockjobbers of the past, the dealers have to enter the trade in the Stock Exchange Automated Quotation System (SEAQ) of alpha—the most actively traded—stocks. Traders and brokers access the information through LSE's electronic service. In the United States, Nasdaq provides a computerized link between buyers and sellers of stocks. The National Association of Securities Dealers (NASD) is a self-regulatory body of brokers and dealers. Much of the trading in Tokyo is done through the Computer Assisted Trading System (CATS).

Theoretically, stock prices are determined by free interaction of market forces, without external interference. In practice, it does not work by the book. On many occasions, patterns of stock prices, to quote Jacobs, "seem to fly in the face of rational pricing and market efficiency."[43] Therefore, efficient market theory (EMT), which

43 Jacobs, 85.

assumes that investors always act rationally, is a fallacy. Stock markets have suffered setbacks due to frantic mob behavior. This is not restricted to individual investors, who have insufficient information and researched material at their disposal, but extends to institutional investors too. Share prices are determined neither by the classical theory of supply and demand nor by the net asset value per share. Rather, the sheer mood, speculation, and irrational behavior of investors cause fluctuations in share prices. The following quote provides a glimpse of how investors behave in the market:

> I'm surrounded by people who are all buying Vodafone in the wake of the AirTouch announcement [talks with AirTouch of the United States for merger]. We all think it is expensive, but we've got to buy it to maintain our weighting in the sector. The more we buy it, the more the price rises, so we have to buy more. Worse of all is that in order to release funds to buy Vodafone, we're having to sell really good small-company shares that are flat on their backs and, of course, as we sell, we drive the prices down further.[44]

In reality, not only the investor expectations dictating the daily movement of prices change, but economic and financial conditions also change. Each boom-and-bust cycle is dictated by different sets of conditions.[45] Because there are numerous variable factors to consider, there are no correct answers. Although investment expertise is available in the market, investors have been aggravated by "deplorable cases of dishonesty and incompetence at some of the largest and best-known city firms."[46] These giant firms or investment houses cause the movement of prices on the market through their voluminous dealings.

Heller writes that as money is pumped into the equity market by rich investors in the West, companies do not know what to do with excess funds, except to allow the prices of shares to fluctuate freely in the market.[47] Normally, the viability of any capital project is preceded by a feasibility study. But this is not always the case. Heller's contention is that even the sophisticated investor is susceptible to irrational behavior.

---

44 "Tomorrow's Giants," February 1999, a sequel to the Treasury's Small Quoted Companies report published in November 1998.

45 Morris, xiv.

46 Davis, 4.

47 Heller, 11–12.

Therefore, "any argument for investing in equities that is based on reason is bound to fail, sooner if not later."[48] He enlists all the excuses that were offered for the market disasters of the 1970s, including the Watergate scandal, the issuance of insurance policies, "over sixty-four thousands of which didn't exist" at all, the issuance of fake death certificates of people who had never even been born, and bankruptcies of stockbrokers because of negligence and gross incompetence.[49] He quotes some examples of how a booming stock can be reduced to ashes within a short span of time. One such example is that Ross Perot's Electronic Data Systems stock rose to $162 in March 1970, turning Perot into a multimillionaire. It then dropped to $12 within four years.[50] Heller also refutes the idea that high fliers always have to fly high. His article "Why High Fliers Fall" demonstrates that even the most popular shares, like IBM, Polaroid, Avon, Disney, McDonald's, Merck, and Xerox, have suffered setbacks.[51]

48 Ibid., 15.
49 Ibid., 16.
50 Ibid., 17.
51 Ibid., 78–79.

CHAPTER 3

HISTORICAL BACKGROUND OF STOCK MARKET BOOMS AND BUSTS

In 1636, the demand for tulips overwhelmed the stock exchange in Holland, dominated by the "gambling mania" of stockjobbers,[52] who dealt on the floor of the exchange. The rush of crowds toward tulip marts was like "flies around a honey pot." From nobles to chimney sweepers, people liquidated their assets and sold their properties to invest in tulips! As prices shot up, investors doubted that they would ever witness poverty. When demand subsided and the masses were stuck with valueless stocks, the courts refused to intervene because "debts contracted in gambling were no debts in law."[53] Tulipomania had spread to England and Paris as well. The Dutch economy faced total collapse. Beckman writes, "Greed and avarice seem to have no boundaries and a most defective memory."[54] The Dutch experience was forgotten, and in 1720, the stock market crashed in France.[55]

In Britain, a 1697 Act of Parliament introduced licensing regulation for stockbrokers and stockjobbers to curb large-scale abuse in market rigging. The license cost two pounds, and the licensee was required to take a solemn oath that he would "truly and faithfully execute and perform the office and employment of a broker...without fraud and collision."[56] The coffeehouses at Change Alley, where dealings used to take place, thrived for almost fifty years. By 1720, the Alley was a source of attraction for lords and ladies as the word spread that share price of the South Sea Company had risen from

52 Mackay, 93–94.

53 Ibid., 95–96.

54 Beckman, 12.

55 *NBK*, 455. Paris Bourse was founded in 1724.

56 Chapman, 11.

£128 to £1,050 within a few months. The purpose of the company was to promote trade with South America and to relieve the government of its debt burden of £9 million. Therefore, the government had a vested interest for encouraging speculation. During eight years, the company was able to win only one contract that to supply black slaves to Latin America.[57]

The British economy faced disaster when the South Sea bubble burst. The South Sea Company—"the Earl of Oxford's masterpiece"—was formed in 1711. The share price had shot up 1,000 percent.[58] Fictitious stocks were issued and ministers were bribed.[59] Corruption swept the nation[60] that was involved in "speculative follies of all time."[61] This compelled Britain to pass the 1720 Bubble Act.[62] In France the country was facing economic catastrophe. Poverty spread like wildfire. During the winter of 1709, "it had been reported that people had been driven to eating human flesh—the corpses [were] found lying on the streets of Paris."[63]

Colin Chapman writes that the first-ever bear market[64] hit London only after the prime minister Sir Robert Walpole (1676–1745), the Prince of Wales, the Duke of Argyll, the chancellor of the exchequer, and many MPs had sold their stocks when prices were at their peak. Within eight weeks the share prices tumbled. The same old reason, which was to feature prominently in the twentieth and twenty-first centuries, was found to be the main culprit—falsification of accounts. The Chancellor of the Exchequer could not enjoy his capital gain of £800,000 as he was sent to the gallows. He was found guilty for the "most notorious, dangerous and infamous corruption."[65] It took about a century for the stock market to revive. However, between 1720 and 1824, the wounds healed and the agony was forgotten, and there was an uninformed new generation on the scene to be targeted. The Depression ended in 1824. The Duke

57 Ibid., 14.

58 Mackay, 65.

59 Ibid., 81.

60 Ibid., 78.

61 Beckman, 12.

62 Morris, 37.

63 Beckman, 26.

64 A bear is an investor or speculator who sells stocks, anticipating a fall in prices. A bear market is one where the trend is of falling stock prices.

65 Chapman, 15.

of Wellington was vehemently opposed to developing railroads under the pretext that "rail roads will only encourage the lower classes to move about needlessly," to quote Chapman.[66]

France was facing economic crisis on a mammoth scale. There was no way that the country could honor its suffocating debts. John Law, a celebrated Scotsman with a criminal record, came to rescue the French economy. He enjoyed the status of being the great-great-nephew of the archbishop of Glasgow. From the pulpit of the royal court, he advocated that the country's prosperity depended on the amount of money in circulation.[67] He was granted a royal decree to establish a bank in his name, which later was converted into Royal Bank of France.[68] Law's promissory notes sold at 15 percent premium whereas Louis XIV's promissory notes sold at 78.5 percent discount.

As the bank was now a public institution, the king ordered issue of notes worth one billion livres without any backing.[69] Investors demanded redemption of notes in gold and silver coins, which the bank could not honor, and it collapsed. But the Mississippi conglomerates, another brainchild of Law, thrived. There was a popular frenzy of buying Mississippi stock. The rent in the vicinity of the market increased sixteen fold. Law made a fortune and lost everything as confidence in the currency and stocks totally eroded. The country stood on the verge of bankruptcy. Yet Law, who was despised in Europe, was invited by the tsar of Russia in 1720 to rescue the Russian economy.[70] He refused and died in poverty.

In Britain, a new regulatory regime was in the offing. Around 1748, the broking firms moved to Threadneedle Street. A six-pence-a-day entrance fee was charged—sufficient to deter the entry of "money-lenders and the other parasites."[71] Commensurate with unprecedented post–Industrial Revolution development, market failures featured in major economies.

The Wall Street was instrumental in US economic growth, yet it was also a center for "scandals, avarice and greed."[72] The post–Civil War crash of 1873 in the United

66 Ibid., 16.

67 Beckman, 30–31.

68 Mackay, 12.

69 Ibid., 11–12.

70 Beckman, 44.

71 Chapman, 18.

72 Geisst, ix.

States lasted six years, and the effects of the crash of 1892–93 were felt for several years.[73] In Chicago, residential land values fell by 85 percent in a period of five years to 1904.[74]

In Germany, confidence in the currency was lost by 1923.[75] Beckman asserts: "In 1923, at the height of inflation, 6430 dogs found their way to the dining tables of the German people."[76] Struck by extreme poverty, the Germans resorted to excessive gambling and drug taking.[77]

In the 1920s, Wall Street was being rated as an "evil in the land."[78] The fear materialized, and the major crash that left its landmark in the history of NYSE was on its way. This was followed by the Great Depression of the thirties.

73 Morris, 49.
74 Beckman, 89.
75 Ibid., 113.
76 Ibid., 118.
77 Ibid., 120.
78 Ibid., 71.

CHAPTER 4

THE GREAT STOCK MARKET CRASH OF 1929

The prelude to the crash was an unregulated financial industry. There was no legal protection for investors against deception by unscrupulous stockbrokers and bankers. Prior to the crash, trust banks loaned large amounts to brokers, who in turn lent them to speculators. Thus, a pyramid of debts was built, as a result of which the market rose by 200 percent between 1925 and 1928.[79] Professor Galbraith draws a vivid picture of how unsecured loans were obtained from commercial banks. When one loan became due, unscrupulous borrowers replaced it with another. The shares of National City Bank had jumped to $2,000 in January 1929. They were selling at $785 per share a year earlier. Charles Mitchell, a senior officer at the bank, earned $1 million a year in bonuses.[80]

By August 1929, Wall Street had become the city's largest tourist-gathering point. When dealers arrived, they were applauded.[81] Their speculations, together with astrologers' predictions, were playing wonders until October 1929, when the bubble finally burst. "Few man-made events, short of the World Wars, created much pain and bitterness, and the fear it could occur again."[82]

Galbraith cites an interesting case of Richard Whitney. He used securities of clients as collateral for his personal debts. His influence with House of Morgan, which was notorious in giving lavish gifts to very special clients, enabled him to borrow $590,000.[83] He lost it all in gambling. Whitney's identity was connected with

79 Geisst, 158, 175.

80 Ibid., 181.

81 Ibid., 186–87.

82 Thomas and Morgan-Witts, xiv.

83 Ibid., 8.

stock exchange, which was considered "the symbolic center of sin." As president of the exchange in 1932, when his own larceny was quite advanced, Whitney publicly appealed for honesty and responsibility of stockbrokers. In April 1932, Whitney was summoned to Senate hearings to answer for malpractice at the NYSE. On April 11, 1938, he was put on trial for grand larceny and was set free on parole after serving only two years' prison sentence.[84]

In the years leading to the crash, the scenario that prevailed was that of financial intrigue, fraud, and the power of big money. Financial houses were flexing their muscles to play a greater role in US business and politics. Until the Federal Reserve Act was passed in 1913, Morgan & Co. enjoyed a "*de facto* status as America's central bank," to the extent that a cry came from Moscow that "Morgan capitalism was trying to run the world."[85]

In the first six months of 1929, 346 banks collapsed in the United States.[86] Underwriters were bribed to raise colossal loans for ruthless dictators and criminals.[87] The son of the president of Peru was paid remuneration of $450,000 for his role in raising a loan of $50 million on Wall Street in 1927. Peru had an internal and external bad-debt problem and was considered a high political risk. Despite this fact, the National City Company floated three successive loan stocks of $15 million and $50 million, followed by $25 million, within months. The loans were not recoverable because the chief negotiator, President Leguia of Peru, was violently removed from office. Chase Bank authorized a generous personal loan to President Machado, the tyrant of Cuba, because of the influence peddling of his son-in-law, who worked for the bank. In this way, the corruption was at its zenith.

On October 24, 1929, thirteen million shares changed hands with orders "to sell at any price." Hysterical crowds gathered on Wall Street. T. B. Lamont, senior partner at J. P. Morgan, assured the mob that the problem was "technical rather than fundamental." The "get-rich-quick schemes" cost $50 billion in losses on October 29, 1929—the day the bubble burst.[88] Eleven speculators committed suicide on that day.[89] When

84 Ibid., 404–5.

85 Ibid., 25.

86 Galbraith, 197.

87 Ibid., 81.

88 Thomas and Morgan-Witts, 384.

89 Mercer, 383.

visitors booked hotel rooms in Manhattan, they were asked whether they wanted a room for accommodation or for jumping out of the window.

Within a few hours on the morning of October 29, the entire year's profits were washed away by losses. Between that date and November 13, $30 billion was wiped out of the US economy. Only two days before the crash, economics professor Irving Fisher of Yale University issued statements, predicting a boom and a continuous growth in the stock market![90]

Buying on margin was an acute problem leading to the crash. Under margin trading, large blocks of shares are bought by putting down a deposit of as little as 3 to 10 percent. The speculator expects that when the shares are sold, there will be a large-enough gain to repay the rest of the money borrowed from the brokers, after covering interest payable. This proved to be a very risky venture. The shares did not rise, but calls were made to repay the debts. By the time investors realized what was happening, the market was recording losses in the billions. The banks that lost their assets dragged their own businesses into the ditch, and their clients with them.

On the expectation that the stock market was "about to climb to the moon,"[91] a syndicate of embezzlers was formed at the Union Industrial Bank in Michigan, where the biggest bank fraud in history (up to that point in time) was planned and executed in 1929. Cashiers and trusted officers pocketed the cash deposited at their counters, which they lost in speculation.[92]

In the Great Depression of the thirties, the US dollar was devalued by 40 percent against gold. The American economy fell downhill into deflation, which came to an end after leaving a memorable casualty in the banking world. More than ten thousand banks declared bankruptcy. They had to pay a heavy price for bad credit given for excessive speculation. Relations between the White House and Wall Street were strained during the Great Depression. Democrats believed that bankers were a "national liability and a danger to democracy."[93] Despite the fact that regulatory laws were passed between 1933 and 1935, public confidence in Wall Street was at its ebb

90 Irving Fisher, Wikipedia Encyclopaedia, https://en.wikipedia.org/wiki/Irving_Fisher.

91 Thomas and Morgan-Witts, 89.

92 Ibid., 84–89.

93 Geisst, 197–98.

for the rest of the decade.[94] Leaders of future political dynasties, like Joseph Kennedy and John Rockefeller, survived the crash.[95] Winston Churchill was present as a speculator in the gallery of the NYSE on the day of the crash[96] and returned home to play a dominant role in world politics.

Mathew Josephson's book *The Robber Barons* was published in 1934. The same year also saw the establishment of the Securities and Exchange Commission (SEC), which is the regulatory and watchdog organization in the US financial world. Financiers and industrialists were blamed for the crash. The book portrayed "capitalism's dark side." It probed into the history of famous financiers like J. P. Morgan, Vanderbilt, and the great fraudster Gould. Morgan had undertaken railroad and US Steel financing and built a financial empire in the process.[97] Vanderbilt, Rockefeller, and J. P. Morgan were very much active in those times and partook in devising ethics for the financial industry.[98] The SEC was given strong regulatory power following a Congressional committee's findings that "stock manipulation on a large scale, blatant dishonesty, and insider trading" were taking place.[99]

A number of corrective measures were adopted to revive the market. Taxes were reduced to put money in the public's pockets, with the aim of stimulating demand. Interest rates were cut.[100] Almost seventy years thereafter, the George W. Bush administration was to adopt the same measures amid corporate scandals that were wrecking public confidence. A member of the SEC summed up the sentiments prevailing after the 1929 crash in his speech at the University of Chicago: "The financial and industrial world has been afflicted with termites...Instead of feeding on wood, they feed and thrive on other people's money."[101]

A University of Melbourne research paper into the causes of the crash identifies polarization between income groups: "The 1 percent of the population at the

94 Ibid., 244.

95 Ibid., 407–8.

96 Ibid., 344.

97 Morris, 53, 57.

98 Andrew Hill, "Rethinking Rockefeller and the Rest," FT.com, July 30, 2002, http://financialtimes.Printthis.Clickability.com.

99 Chapman, 169.

100 Geisst, 196.

101 Ibid., 248.

very top of the pyramid had incomes 650 percent greater than those 11 percent of the Americans at the bottom of the pyramid."[102] Mergers caused competition and buoyancy in the economy to disappear. Many of the newly established banks were insolvent; there was no regulation requiring them to maintain minimum capital and reserves. US exports were badly hit with protectionist policies. The Republican administration of President Herbert Hoover had to take major blame, although he had warned of the impending dangers of speculation. But investors saw the stock market as a stepping-stone to jump quickly into prosperity.

In a strong bull market[103] of 1954–69, political uncertainty, a decline in the value of the dollar, rising oil prices, and rising inflation[104] pulled interest rates "to their highest levels in American history."[105] The dollar was losing purchasing power. The United States faced budget deficits, and Britain faced a chronic problem with balance of payments.[106] Britain blamed international speculators for devaluation of the sterling.[107] In 1971, the United States devalued the dollar and prohibited its convertibility into gold. In 1975, New York City faced bankruptcy.[108] The scene was set for the bear market of 1970–81. All of these factors combined to trigger the great crash of 1987.

Amid turmoil over the hike in oil prices after the 1973 Arab-Israeli war, the net effect of the hazardous acceleration in oil prices, as it was seen, was the unceremonious increase of $80 billion petrodollars in the coffers of the banks.[109]

Heller dedicates a chapter in his book to disprove the belief that investment in stocks and shares is a hedge against inflation. He gives the example of research conducted in 1975 by Irvin Friend and Marshall Blume of the Wharton School of Finance in the United States. They found no evidence at all in their research, over a period of

---

102 "The 1929 Stock Market Crash," University of Melbourne, Business.com, http://www.arts.unimelb.edu.au/amu/ucr/. (converted into digitalized collection).

103 A bull is an investor or speculator who buys stocks, anticipating a rise in stock prices. A bull market is one in which there is a trend of rising stock prices.

104 Inflation is a percentage increase in the prices of goods and services, reflecting depletion in the purchasing power of a currency.

105 Geisst, 300.

106 Balance of payments is the net financial balance of total receipts and total payments to foreign countries from transactions of goods, services, and investments.

107 Geisst, 302.

108 Ibid., 313.

109 Strange, 18.

forty years, between inflation and stock market performance.[110] He reflects on misleading and grossly exaggerated advertisements that succeeded in luring investors to part with their money. The vulnerable investors "fell for stories...like the British fund operator who placed excessive loads of his investors' loot into a palpably nonexistent California gold mine."[111]

110 Heller, 41.
111 Ibid., 51.

CHAPTER 5

THE STOCK MARKET CRASHES OF THE SEVENTIES

Describing the tumultuous events of the mid-1970s on the American Stock Exchange, and on the world's stock markets in general, Robert Heller[112] refers to the "biggest con" to which the investing public had fallen because "so large an army of deceivers told the tale and took the slice of the action."[113] And what was the result? It was like taking inventory of the property in Hiroshima after the bomb.[114] But then, "stockbrokers, tipsters, bankers, hot-shot salesmen, mandarins, economists, promoters, managers, journalists, and politicians" were involved in intense speculation.[115] Heller also refutes the myth that stock prices are directly related to asset value. He gives an example that DuPont, in this period, sold its assets for twice the price of their total worth.[116] This means that the price is determined according to investors' expectations about the future, which may prove to be totally erroneous.

The Great Stock Market Crash of 1987

From the beginning of 1987 up to August 25, the DJIA[117] climbed by 826 points, or 43.6 percent.[118] On October 16, it fell by 500 points. On October 19, it suffered the

112 An experienced journalist who worked for *Investor's Guardian* and the London *Observer.*

113 Heller, 4.

114 Ibid., 2.

115 Ibid., 4.

116 Ibid., 6–7.

117 The Dow Jones Industrial Index consists of thirty major US stocks quoted on the NYSE. It is named after Charles Dow, the first editor of the *Wall Street Journal*. It measures the trend of the stock market. Another important index on the NYSE is the S&P 500 Index. It consists of five hundred stocks chosen on the basis of size, liquidity, and type of sector. It is a market-value weighted index of the five hundred representative corporations.

118 Jacobs, 69.

worst fall of 508 points, or 22.6 percent up to that point in time. On the NYSE, 604 million shares changed hands, to the value of $21 billion. On October 20, the FTSE lost more than 20 percent of its value.[119] More than 39 million shares changed hands at British Petroleum alone.[120] Between August 25 and October 20, the DJIA had lost 1,000 points, or 37 percent.[121] The epicenter of the crash was New York, which dragged the world markets to doom. But James Baker, the US treasury secretary at the time, said, "The Reagan administration saw no cause for panic," according to Jacobs.

Researchers differ in their findings on whether the 1987 crash should be construed as rational or irrational behavior of investors to restore equilibrium,[122] which cannot be determined with certainty. Sentiments and perceptions of investors and their overreaction to imperfect information in imperfect market conditions were some of the factors that led to the crash. The part played by the rule of thumb in the rising market was also significant as investors made impulsive decisions.

The Brady Commission appointed by President Reagan found "unprecedented futures discounts" as the cause for depressing the markets.[123] The wave of sell orders that hit the market on the day of the crash made the market "highly illiquid," and the margin between the bid price and the ask price disappeared.[124] Telephone lines were jammed, and brokers avoided answering phone calls. Panic followed, and the NYSE suspended dealings in the afternoon of the following day, hoping the market would stabilize. Other factors also played a background role in provoking the crash.

Throughout the 1970s and early 1980s, London gained popularity in Eurodollar[125] deposits and later the Eurobonds[126] market. It succeeded in attracting money from the Organization of Petroleum Exporting Countries (OPEC). "Saudi Arabia alone had over $50 billion deposited in the European banks."[127] This was trivial in comparison to

---

119 Chapman, 187.

120 Ibid., 188.

121 Jacobs, 69–71.

122 Ibid., 96–97.

123 Ibid., 111.

124 Ibid., 115.

125 Eurodollars are deposits issued by banks outside the United States.

126 Eurobonds are issued in different currencies outside the domestic capital market, underwritten by a banking syndicate.

127 Geisst, 1997, 310–12.

$800 billion in Saudi investments[128] and total Arab investments of $3.5 trillion[129] in the United States by August 2002.

In 1982, the end of the recession created a strong rally in the stock markets, owing to takeover activities. The tactic used was to issue junk bonds at a higher-than-average interest rate. These bonds were secured on the shares of the company being targeted. In case the bidder failed to control the company, he or she could still end up with a worthwhile capital gain by selling shares, which would have risen on speculation.[130] By 1989, $201 billion worth of junk bonds were sold on the markets.[131] Junk bonds had littered the market to the extent that, despite the fact that countries like Cuba had floated them on the market, the speculators bet that they were bound to fetch value on a change of leadership.[132]

Michael Milken, the "king of junk bonds," amassed $3 billion in personal wealth and $550 million in bonuses, which made him "the country's highest-paid executive."[133] The boom saw enhanced activity in takeovers and mergers, whose value reached $300 billion a year.[134] When Kohlberg Kravis Roberts & Co. (KKP) acquired Beatrice in 1985 for $5.6 billion, Milken was issued with warrants, which he sold "for one hundred times their value."[135] Milken's investment bank, Drexel, confessed that insider information on the takeover was passed to Ivan F. Boesky, who was convicted and sentenced to three and a half years in prison in 1987. But he made a deal with Rudolf Giuliani, the US attorney for the Southern District of New York at the time. As a result, he was released after serving half of his sentence and paying a $100 million penalty. Milken was indicted on one hundred counts of fraud in March 1990. Yet he was hailed as a "financial genius."[136] Experts believe that junk bonds paved the way for the imminent stock market crash because their promoters were in the business of squandering the funds of investors.

---

128 As reported on Al Jazeera TV on August 22, 2002.

129 As reported on ANN TV on September 22, 2002.

130 Chapman, 144.

131 Ibid., 144.

132 Geisst, 335.

133 Chapman, 337.

134 Ibid., 339.

135 Ibid., 341.

136 Ibid., 358.

The NYSE triggered worldwide falls on October 19, 1987, wiping out more than $1 trillion dollars from US share values within minutes. In London, £50 billion was wiped out from share values. Nigel Lawson, the British Chancellor of the Exchequer at that time, called the crash the "nonevent of the year."[137] Sydney lost one-quarter of its value, and Tokyo fell by one-fifth. The crash was blamed on US trade and budget deficits, a hike in interest rates, and computer trading.[138] This time, a number of stock-brokers resorted to committing suicide rather than facing their clients, whom they had grossly misled and ruined financially.

The United States is the largest debtor nation in the world. It runs trade deficits because its imports exceed its exports. It runs budget deficits because its current and capital spending exceeds its revenues.[139] The 1987 crash, called Black Monday, was twice as bad in percentage terms[140] as the 1929 crash, Black Tuesday.[141] Ironically, the market losses were reflected in phenomenal profit figures of the five hundred largest American corporations, which reported an increase in revenues exceeding $2 trillion.

Christopher Wood describes the malpractice that prevailed then of using tokkin funds to accumulate shares. A *tokkin* is a fund or investment company owned by a Japanese corporation (other than a financial services company). A tokkin invests in speculative, often high-risk securities in Japanese companies. In order to lure investors to invest in ultra-risky securities, false information about high performance of the securities was given to the press. Manipulation extended to feeding false stories to the press until there was a large-enough profit to sell. "In such ramps, an obscure share can double or triple in a matter of weeks."[142] The lending policy of big American banks was heading for trouble. Wood writes that for every dollar American banks lent at home, they lent six- or sevenfold offshore. Consequently, on March 31, 1987, "the offshore Eurocurrency deposit market totaled $3.85 trillion...This was money outside the world's national banking system."[143]

---

137 Beckman, 211.

138 Mercer, 1290.

139 Bose, 151.

140 Wood, 2.

141 Thomas and Morgan-Witts, 384.

142 Wood, 62.

143 Ibid., 82.

Heller writes, "The offshore groups can justifiably argue that they merely carried on the good work of the onshore investment Mafia."[144] If the loot was engineered in one of the dubious offshore centers, then the fund managers ensured that "every one of the fraudulent or quasi-fraudulent operations had trustees and bankers of impeccable pedigree, bearing, and repute."[145]

These groups even hired public figures to act as chairmen for the funds. In this way, the investor's attention could successfully be diverted from the dubious and insider dealings of the funds. The investor remained under the false impression, as intended by fund managers, that no person or organization of repute could possibly lend its name to a venture that might damage its reputation. Evidently, all the custodians and auditors of the dubious offshore funds were concerned about was earning colossal fees and charges.

To protect their professional reputation, even if the auditors had to qualify their reports in the final accounts, they chose vague and misleading wording. Heller describes the role played by reputable bankers and famous firms of auditors whose primary concern was to absolve themselves from any responsibility "behind the smoke screen of words."[146]

Lack of regulation was the essential characteristic of the Eurobond market. This defect was aggravated by speculative instruments, which were called "perpetual floating-rate notes." These did not have to be repaid by borrowers. Instead, interest was paid in perpetuity as the instruments changed hands. Such instruments became very attractive for banks because they could remain in circulation forever, and the banks did not have to worry about repaying the debts.[147] Prior to the crash of 1987, $18 billion worth of floating-rate notes were issued, of which $12 billion was held by Japanese banks. Those banks bore a loss of $1.5 billion.

Wood discusses the problem of massive outstanding debts in the bond market, which set the scene for the crash. The New York investment house Salomon Brothers grew by 40 percent in 1986. A week before the 1987 crash, it laid off 12 percent of its workforce. Municipal-bond traders at Salomon Brothers earned an annual salary

144 Heller, 8.

145 Ibid., 52.

146 Ibid., 53.

147 Wood, 84–85.

of $300,000, which indicates the extent of the frenzy in the bond market. In 1987, America's long-term government bond market was worth $17 billion. Outstanding Treasury bond futures were worth $22 billion. In Tokyo, the daily average spot trading in yen government bonds reached $20 billion, and the bond-futures market climbed to $46 billion, according to Wood. The market became saturated, and the demand could not be sustained.

In the aftermath of the 1987 crash, market efficiency theory was criticized. Under this maxim, security prices are supposed to reflect all publicly available information, excluding unexpected changes in the economy or specific corporate information.[148] Factors affecting the US economy were scrutinized. Fear of inflation, the weakening dollar, and the impact of a rise in oil prices were among the variables that came under close examination.[149] Volatility was also attributed to a change from a fixed to a floating rate of exchange.[150] It was noticed that insurers reacted to price movements within minutes, while value investors were slow and reacted within days.[151]

The 1987 crash marked the end of the five-year bull market. The problem of liquidity in the market was partly solved when the Federal Reserve pumped in $2.2 billion by purchasing back government securities. That is why the US economy did not drift into recession, in contrast with the 1929 crash. However, fifteen thousand employees were laid off on Wall Street.[152]

The crash left its footprints on the New Zealand Exchange as well. Following the deregulation of the financial industry, stock prices tripled between 1984 and 1987. After the crash of 1987 up until the 1990s, fraud squads were engaged heavily in unresolved criminal activities of "phony real estate transactions."[153] In 1984, New Zealand owed about 47 percent of its gross domestic product in foreign debts, which increased to 90 percent by 1993.[154] Private companies owed NZ $22 billion in 1989 in foreign

---

148 Jacobs, 76.

149 Ibid., 78–79.

150 Ibid., 110.

151 Ibid., 126.

152 "The 1987 Stock Market Crash," University of Melbourne, Business.com, http://www.arts.unimelb.edu.au/amu/ucr/. (converted into digitalized collection).

153 Engler, 141.

154 Ibid., 142.

debts, which increased to NZ $40 billion in 1992.[155] Thus, the aftereffects of the crash were felt for several years.

One of the reasons for the crash, as explored by Jegadeesh and Titman (1993), was that investors were tempted to "buy past winners and sell past losers, causing prices to overreact."[156] The crash gave rise to an economic slump, which was caused by the decline in demand. This in turn resulted in a spiral of decline in production and a rise in unemployment. To stimulate demand, the interest rate was reduced, which may have given rise to inflation. The average price-earnings ratio (P/E)[157] of US stocks prior to the 1929 crash was 60; prior to the 1987 crash, it was 25. The P/E of Japanese stocks had been 50, reflecting how the stocks were generally overvalued.[158]

155 Ibid., 143.

156 Jacobs, 86.

157 This means the number of years' worth of that year's earnings investors are prepared to pay for investing in the shares of the company.

158 "The 1987 Stock Market Crash," University of Melbourne, Business.com. n.d. (converted into digitalized collection).

CHAPTER 6

THE STOCK MARKET CRASHES OF THE NINETIES

The cycle of market decline was repeated in October 1989, November 1991, October 1997, August 1998,[159] and August 2000. On the tenth anniversary of the 1987 crash, the DJIA had more than quadrupled, with mutual funds recording a growth from $200 billion to more than $2 trillion. This hyperactivity in the market led many investors to make rash decisions unsupported by economic fundamentals. The sensitivity of the market can be observed from a few incidences. On July 23, 1998, Federal Reserve Board chairman Alan Greenspan told Congress, "Stock price levels are too high." In quick reaction, stock prices started to fall. As President Clinton started to testify on August 17 in the Monica Lewinsky furor, the market became jubilant and rallied. The market mood is at times closely related to politicians' mood. The Republican victory in the American presidential election of 2000 was interpreted as good for the market. When the deadlock occurred in the ballot count or the alleged vote rigging in Florida, this was interpreted as bad for the market. The market does not like uncertainties, but certainty is a rare commodity in the modern world.

The entire financial industry sits on an iceberg of risks, which, in the process of melting, sends investors straight into the sea. Even bonds, which are considered relatively less risky than equities, carry a high risk of the borrower either not being able to meet interest payments according to the terms and conditions of the issued bonds or not being able to honor the repayment of principal. Nobody can guarantee that the borrower or the issuer of bonds, no matter how giant and internationally reputable, will not default. The credit rating agencies in the market are as imperfect as the

159 Jacobs, 6.

market itself. Government bonds are risk-free because governments can print money to honor their commitments; private and public institutions cannot.

Sometimes, without any economic justification, the stock market climbs a cliff until the market becomes saturated. Then the market takes a deep dive into the sea because it rose on the basis of rumors in the first place. In this way, the investments of thousands of investors are washed away simply because they trusted the untrustworthy system at their peril. These investors were not aware of the rules of the game. If the godfathers of the usurious racketeering could have gotten a listing on the stock market, they would not have hesitated to float shares to deal in body parts and human remains. Such is the ferocity of greed in a system that makes billionaires out of the misery of unaware, innocent investors or members of the public who have dumped their savings into the system through pension or mutual funds or direct investment in shares and stocks.

The circumstances that caused all the major crashes were different from those that caused a number of minicrashes in the nineties. In October 1989, over-the-counter (OTC) put options—risk hedging—were valued at $2 billion.[160] As the market fell, the brokers who had written the puts were the first to sell. Selling the hedge in the declining market proved as disastrous as in 1987. On November 15, 1991, the SEC reported that market falls on that day were similar to the declines on October 1989. The bulk of market-on-close (MOC) orders were processed by the derivatives.[161]

Between 1985 and 1991, the "Turkish stock market rose more than 3000 percent, Chile by over 2800 percent, and Mexico by nearly 2000 percent."[162] The economies of these countries were in tatters. Yet speculative frenzy had taken over and was heading toward an inevitable bust. The unscrupulous stockbrokers were prone to tell their clients that the stocks were constantly on the rise, but they were less likely to disclose the colossal risk involved of losing the capital altogether in these types of investments.

Between 1980 and 1995, market capitalization of twenty-four emerging markets expanded by 1,200 percent, and stock dealings widened by 1,900 percent.[163] This growth could not be sustained, and the market had to fall. Financial barons in the

160 Ibid., 215.

161 Ibid., 218.

162 Davis, 197.

163 Ibid., 198.

main market centers also played their part. According to *Globe and Mail*, nine families owned stock values equivalent to 50 percent of the quoted companies on the Toronto Stock Exchange.[164]

Fisher Black (1996) introduced the concept of noise in the market. Noise is produced when investors "err in the same direction"[165] and base their investment decisions solely on price movements.[166] "Feedback" investors trade on the basis of price fluctuations[167] rather than major economic news.[168] Noise is to be distinguished from informative signals.[169]

Several factors contributed to the boom of the eighties, including the abolishment of exchange controls, capital mobility at the click of a button, and deregulation of financial systems.[170] Within two years of the 1987 crash, Tokyo emerged as the star performer, with the Nikkei exceeding thirty-eight thousand points. But recurring scandals involving members of the government rocked the TSE, while the Nikkei started falling sharply. In 1990, within a year, Tokyo's market had fallen by 40 percent, wiping out $2 trillion from the share values.[171]

At the peak of the bull market in the 1980s, when the Japanese company Nippon Telephone and Telegraph (NTT) was privatized, each share sold at $1,700. By mid-1992, NTT shares had fallen by more than 80 percent.[172] Jim Jubak warned in 1996 that the risk-reward ratio was not in favor of investors. He wrote, "So don't buy on future earnings. Don't pay for stories. Don't chase hot stocks. And don't forget history."[173] Between 1987 and 1997, the DJIA climbed 400 percent. There was no justification for this bull market from the perspective of corporate earnings or the GDP. Neither of the two rose proportionately with the stock market. Investors were once again ignoring economic fundamentals. The United States was facing an acute budget deficit,

---

164 Engler, 60, quoting Dan Westell, "Big Chunk of Business in Hands of a Few," *Globe and Mail*, August 25, 1984.

165 Jacobs, 87.

166 Ibid., 121.

167 Ibid., 90.

168 Ibid., 91.

169 Ibid., 99.

170 Warburton, 70.

171 Quoting *Newsweek*, (American weekly news), October 15, 1990.

172 Chapman, 49.

173 Jim Jubak, "96/10—Crash Testing," www.Business.com, October 1996.

and the dollar was persistently weakening. The dollar had to be supported through the intervention of European central banks, which bought US currency in the open market to create an artificial drain in supply. Yet it remained weak against the German mark and the Japanese yen.

The strength of the yen negatively affected Japanese exports to the United States. This factor combined with other factors, such as corruption and irrecoverable bank loans, to hit the Japanese market hard. The result was that the Nikkei floated below ten thousand points, a level it had reached more than twenty years earlier. A writer for the *Financial Times* wrote that Japan is "run by a cartel of vested interests and lobby groups."[174]

Nomura Securities, which started as a money exchanger in the back streets of Osaka in 1872, was by now one of the largest securities houses in the world.[175] Business ethics did not go hand in hand with size. This fact was demonstrated in 1997, when Nomura's president admitted to making illegal payments of $50 million to gangsters, who were paid to disrupt the company's annual meetings. Nomura had been convicted of a similar offense in 1991, which cost its revenues $36 million.[176] Bribery and corruption scandals involving top government officials also damaged the reputation of the Japanese markets.

Since the crash of 1997 in the Far East, corruption in corporate behavior in Malaysia was a cause of discontent. Therefore, the bosses of the largest companies agreed to a "voluntary code of corporate governance."[177] But regionally or globally, the problem was the same. Regulators were not given a free hand to enforce the laws. Unless politicians regulated themselves to change their lifestyle of influence peddling, the regulations could not be implemented effectively.

In the Far East, a fifty-one-year-old American-born Bangkok financier, Pin Chakkaphak, was alleged to have triggered the 1997 Asian financial crash. He rightly retorted, "If a financial system can be brought down by one person, there is something very wrong with the system itself."[178]

---

174 "Leader: Trouble in Tokyo," *Financial Times*, October 25, 2002.

175 Chapman, 55.

176 Ibid., 58.

177 John Thornhill, "Corporate Restructuring: Fat Cats Go on a Diet," FT.com, October 17, 2002.

178 Harvey Morris, "'Asian Crash' Case Accused Wins Fight to Stay in UK," *Financial Times*, July 28, 2001.

On October 27, 1997, the DJIA recorded its largest drop of 7 percent, or 554 points, with a share volume of 685 million. The next day, 1.2 billion shares were traded. By this time, OTC options on the US equity index were valued at $200 billion, and exchange-trade options (ETO) were valued at $300 billion.[179] There was an additional risk for OTC holders defaulting to pay. To remedy this deficiency, a clearinghouse was introduced in 1996. This was a secondary market aimed at creating price transparency and a credit guarantee.[180]

The Vancouver Composite Index fell by more than 25 percent in less than six weeks during spring of 1997. The collapse was caused by the failure of Bre-X Miners with their "Indonesian claims" that mining done on "the world's largest gold deposit" proved to be nothing but fraudulent, according to research conducted by William O. Brown Jr. and Richard C. K. Burdekin. The fraud of this scale hit small exploration companies hard as well.[181]

In 1998, the Russian market fell by more than 70 percent.[182] The ruble was devalued, and a moratorium was placed on $40 billion worth of overseas debts. The Soros fund alone reported a $2 billion loss on Russian debts. Part of the blame for the crash of 1998 was placed at the doorstep of Long-Term Capital Management (LTC), whose partners earned a hefty return of 25 percent of gross profit. But they could not stop 44 percent of LTC's capital from being lost, although two of its partners had worked under the former vice chairman of the Federal Reserve Board. Two others had won the Noble Prize in 1997.[183]

The LTC had built a $100 billion portfolio[184] but held a derivatives position with a notional value of $1.25 trillion.[185] This in itself was an invitation for disaster. The market took a turn in the other direction, and the book values of bets on European equity markets became payable. Even after disposing of all their holdings, the option-market

---

179 Jacobs, 220.

180 Ibid., 234.

181 William O. Brown Jr. and Richard C. K. Burdekin, "Fraud and Financial Markets: The 1997 Collapse of the Junior Mining Stocks," Claremont College (California), http://ideas.repec.org/s/clm/clmeco.html. Journal of Economics and Business, Vol. 52, Issue 3, May – June 2000.

182 Jacobs, 276.

183 Ibid., 278–79.

184 Ibid., 292.

185 Ibid., 281.

makers were short $27 billion in stock-index futures on September 11, 1998.[186] A high amount of debts could not be serviced because the interest rate, equity, and bond markets went the opposite way of what was expected.

The liquidation of LTC proved that the system itself was unstable. The regulatory watchdogs relied on the risk assessment of interested parties, such as lenders. This gave way to "a period of uncontrolled credit expansion."[187]

Bond markets were paralyzed.[188] The Federal Reserve had to step in and rescue LTC because seventy-five financial institutions involved as lenders were facing a drain on market liquidity. But the controversy remained regarding whether the Federal Reserve should have intervened to save investors who had undertaken unmanageable risks. LTC's scandal adversely affected global stock markets in the nineties.

186 Ibid., 284.

187 Soros, 119.

188 Jacobs, 284–87, 299.

CHAPTER 7

WEAPONS OF MASS DISTORTIONS

Sometimes fund managers and stockbrokers make incredible claims to prey on naïve and uninformed investors. Here is a hypothetical example: £1,000 invested in XYZ Company in 1930 would be worth more than £1 million in 2030, except that XYZ Company might not have existed in 1930 and in all probability would never see 2030. This is tantamount to making up performance figures and absolving oneself of any responsibility for misrepresentation by printing a disclaimer clause in unreadable small print.

Heller asserts that stockbrokers may be subject to three squeezes. In a bear market, the volume of dealings declines. Thus, the commissions they earn on a percentage basis, whether on price or volume, decline together with the decline in their own investments.[189] In these circumstances, some unscrupulous brokers are tempted to recommend to their clients funds of questionable integrity. Because many, if not most, stockbrokers are limited companies, investors should take precautions by ordering a copy of audited accounts and directors' reports to find out whether the company is financially sound or insolvent.

Heller writes, "Brokers are in much the same position as racehorse tipsters or... promoters of fraudulent investments. If a tipster truly knew which horse was going to win, he would be certifiably insane to pass on the information to the world at large."[190] Many naïve investors rely on tips from brokers to buy, sell, or retain a stock. According to his study, tips can go drastically wrong.

The time to buy and the time to sell became a subjective rather than an objective matter, based on intuition and guess-work. Some professionally run pension funds got

189 Heller, 146.

190 Ibid., 147.

"stuck with shares during the worst year of the Second Great Crash."[191] Heller asserts that investors should have clear and measurable targets in terms of time—the period of time they plan to hold the investment—as well as gain: What is their profit expectation in the set time period? Unless they do so, they are neither wise nor "more sophisticated than a French peasant who buries his coins in the ground."[192]

Sometimes investors are deceived with gimmicks. Heller cites a scenario of an amateur investor who put his family money into certain funds or shares with the sole rationale that so-and-so (a public figure with a title), who acts as chairman of the fund, can look after the investor's family's money better than the investor himself does, just as the chairman has looked after his own family's fortunes! Heller cautions amateur and naïve investors against buying shares just because "the market has been galloping ahead" and they feel like going for a ride. He advises the investor to look into the market capitalization of the fund or company and its past performance but warns that "self-deception is an inherent aberration in the psychology of investment,"[193] not to mention taking stockbrokers' and investment advisors' word on face value.

Boiler Room Scams

Boiler room scams involve targeting gullible consumers and ripping them off through the promotion of shares that are worthless in value. In business, the term "boiler room" refers to an outbound call center selling questionable investments by telephone. It typically refers to a room where salesmen work using unfair, dishonest sales tactics, sometimes selling penny stocks or private placements or committing outright stock fraud. The term carries a negative connotation and is often used to imply high-pressure sales tactics and, sometimes, poor working conditions.[194]

Boiler room fraudsters follow the tactics of cold-calling, for which they adopt techniques of well-trained salesmen and push dubious shares aggressively through unrealistic and false claims of performance. They are very persuasive in convincing investors to part with their money. They do not take no for an answer and keep on

191 Ibid., 150.

192 Ibid., 157.

193 Ibid., 172.

194 Boiler room business, https://en.wikipedia.org/wiki/Boiler_room_(business) *Wikipedia Encyclopedia*

making unsolicited phone calls, usually from overseas call centers, with background voices giving an impression of a busy office taking orders for shares. The best way to recognize them is when they start claiming that under their scheme, the investment is going to double or triple within a short time. It has become much cheaper for share pushers in Europe and the United States to operate call centers from overseas—notably India, where labor comes at a fraction of the cost as at home. The safest way to deal with these rogues is to hang up the phone as soon as they start introducing themselves. Sometimes boiler room callers use the names of genuine firms registered with the Financial Services Authority (FSA), and they may even change their own names frequently.

The City of London Police warns[195] that scams often have similar features that may alert you to the fact that they are not genuine:

1. If it sounds too good to be true, it probably is.
2. You are asked for money up front to pay unexpected fees (such as customs) before your "prize" can be released.
3. You are asked to provide your bank account, credit card details, or other sensitive personal information.
4. You are put under pressure to reply immediately or the money will be given to someone else.
5. You are asked to keep the details secret.

The list of warnings is not exhaustive.

On its website, the FSA publishes a list of unauthorized firms/individuals, unauthorized overseas firms operating in the United Kingdom, unauthorized Internet banks, and a list of notices/warnings issued by other foreign regulatory authorities.[196]

Because of the lax legislation of offshore centers, meant to permit professional criminals and promoters of boiler room shares and investment funds to convert black

195 "International Police Operation Targets Suspected Boiler Room Masterminds." City of London Police, April 3, 2014, https://www.cityoflondon.police.uk/news-and-appeals/international-police-operation-targets-suspected-boiler-room-masterminds.

196 "FCA Campaigns to Protect Public from Investment Fraud," Financial Services Authority, May 26, 2016, http://www.fscs.org.uk/news/2016/may/fca-campaign-to-protect-public-from-investment-fraud/.

money into white, the investor should avoid anything and everything registered in offshore centers, such as those in the Caribbean islands and elsewhere. Even if these companies use the services of internationally reputable banks and auditors, they are not to be trusted. At the end of the day, the bank providing custodial services and the famous auditing firms use the exclusion clauses in small print to save their skins from any litigation if things go wrong—and they are meant to go wrong.

The boiler room schemes started in America, acquired prominence in the United States, Spain, Italy, and Switzerland. In most, if not all, cases, boiler room schemes (see glossary of terms at the end) are not quoted on any stock exchange, so they cannot be sold easily at the investor's will. In the United Kingdom, they are illegal. But this does not stop boiler room criminals from targeting overseas investors by pretending to be based in the United Kingdom. They obtain a database of the shareholders of reputable companies from the register of shareholders and then start chasing them to the point of creating a nuisance with e-mails, phone calls, and mail shots (letters sent by post). They may even run professionally designed websites to give the false impression that they are genuine. Under the Financial Services and Markets Act 2000, financial companies are not supposed to cold-call customers who have not requested their services.

The Role of Portfolio Insurance

The objective of portfolio insurance is to protect against loss of share values in a falling market. Portfolio insurance grew from $4 billion at the end of 1985 to about $80 billion just before the 1987 crash. Between October 14 and 20, 1987, $20 billion to $30 billion worth of shares were offloaded on the market.[197] As a result, portfolio insurance failed to honor the claims.

Between 1982 and 1987, the market rose steadily. A week before the 1987 crash, as soon as the market declined, insured investors started to sell. On the day of the crash, portfolio insurance failed to be a hedge against volatility. Yet as the dust settled, options exchange took over the function of portfolio insurance. In the United States, portfolio insurance was offered beyond US markets on fixed-income securities, commodities, foreign stocks, currencies, and pension funds.[198]

197 Wood, 108–10.
198 Jacobs, 44–46.

Jacobs provides an illustration to show that $1 invested in the S&P 500 index in 1928 would have grown to $104.25 up to 1982 without portfolio insurance. But it would have grown to $52.36 with such protection. Despite a substantial premium cost, this strategy was nullified in the wake of the 1987 crash. Portfolio insurance was meant to protect not the investor's interest but the fund manager's interest. In practice, it failed to protect both.[199] This is because portfolio insurance failed to honor its commitments in a falling market because it had invested clients' premiums in the declining shares.

The US General Accounting Office found in 1988 that portfolio insurance "gave institutional investors a false sense of security, thereby encouraging overinvestment in the stock market."[200] Insurers' belief that the price of stock-index futures tends to follow stock prices proved erroneous. There was a wide gap between the two after the 1987 crash. Futures fell sharply because investors were heading in the same direction. The sale of futures sparked investor hysteria to sell stocks. As the demand for stocks fell, prices fell, dragging futures with them in a vicious cycle of deeper falls. Insurers were the single largest group that sold insurance policies in 1987, in the same way as the margin traders who triggered the crash of 1929.[201] Analysts believed that portfolio theory was the best alternative to portfolio insurance. Portfolio theory advocated diversification or an asset mix, urging investors to ignore short-term market swings and stay with the market on a long-term basis.[202]

199 Ibid., 46–56, 346.

200 Ibid., 138.

201 Ibid., 144, 174.

202 Ibid., 266, quoting *New York Times*, June 15, 1990.

CHAPTER 8

THE GREAT STOCK MARKET MELTDOWN OF THE TWENTY-FIRST CENTURY

Biggs compares and contrasts the overvaluation of real estate and stock prices leading to the boom-and-bust in Japan with the situation in the United States by September 2008. Federal Reserve chairman Ben Bernanke told the Japanese to "flood your economy with liquidity, even if it means dropping money from helicopters."[203] This shows that the authorities bothered only with short-term solutions, not taking into account the untold damage this could do to the economy in the long run.

The Nikkei index peaked at thirty-nine thousand points on December 29, 1989. But when the bubble burst, the Nikkei dropped by 60 percent in a short span of only two years, wiping out all the previous gains. By 2003, it recorded 7,832 points, a drop of 80 percent. Biggs writes that within five and a half years, the Nikkei had climbed by 400 percent as a result of "corporate gambling." He notes that in 1989 in Japan, the price-earnings ratio of the market stood at seventy, whereas the price-to-book value was more than five.[204]

This proves that in the course of gambling by speculators, a scenario is created that is totally divorced from reality, as represented by the figures.

By 2003, when the stock market witnessed a continuous downward spiral, it was recording the worst corporate performance figures in seventy years. The surrender values of pension and endowment policies made investors face a harsh reality: the values of investments are unsecured in both the short term and the long term. In Britain,

203 Barton Biggs, "The Summer of the Discontent: Bernanke Told the Japanese to Boost Liquidity, Even If It Meant Dropping Money from Helicopters," *Newsweek*, vol. 152, no. 11, September 15, 2008.

204 PE ratio or price-to-earnings ratio is an essential stock market measure. To calculate a PE ratio, one simply divides a company's current share price by its latest or predicted earnings per share (EPS). EPS is the slice of the company's after-tax profits every year.

Equitable Life faced imminent liquidation when the House of Lords ordered the company to honor its obligations and pay policyholders the guaranteed policy values. Had it not found a buyer to take over its assets, the company would have been dissolved after more than a century of existence.

The first downward trend of the twenty-first century was initiated by the dotcom and telecom shares meltdown. A three-year boom in the telecom sector came to an abrupt end in March 2000 as the market became totally saturated. The profit warnings from the telecom corporations in the United States and Europe caused the market to collapse. Due to a gloomy picture, many small and institutional investors questioned whether the market was heading toward a bust, or a "correction," as the dealers call it so as to confuse public opinion. The volatility of the telecom shares became apparent as the share prices of Vodafone, the largest company in the United Kingdom, were at a twenty-month low. AT&T saw its value wiped out by 75 percent. The share value of Deutsche Telecom, the largest company in Germany, declined by 60 percent within a year of its part privatization. Cable & Wireless, which had a healthy financial position, came under intense pressure. WorldCom, in the United States, saw its market capitalization dwindle from $150 billion to $50 billion. As a result of the bear market and recession, US pension funds fell by 70 percent.[205]

BT took the lead in breaking its operations into smaller units and selling its UK assets. The change in its strategy was aimed at addressing the debt crisis, which was in the billions of pounds. But almost ten years after the collapse of dotcom and telecom shares, the impact was still very much visible in the share prices of BT, whose shares became penny shares. On the eve of privatization on December 3, 1984, shares in BT were offered to the public at fifty pence per share. The British government's privatization scheme attracted public interest, thanks to an intensive advertising campaign on TV for two months before the floatation of shares. Within two months after floatation, the prices tripled. But the honeymoon came to an end within two more months. The shares started underperforming in the market. Research statistics show that the price of BT shares reached more than eleven pounds a share in 2000. Almost ten years later, they had been so badly battered that they remained at around one pound a share.

---

205 Porter Stansberry, "The Debt Generation," *Daily Reckoning*, Paris, November 27, 2002.

The US telecom giants were facing fierce competition in long-distance calls. In Europe, the problem was different. The colossal cost of acquisition of third-generation mobile licenses resulted in huge debts in the balance sheets of companies like Vodafone, BT, Deutsche Telecom, and France Telecom. Their credit ratings were slashed, and banks were warned against pumping further loans into them. These reputable telecom giants became white elephants. Over a period of almost ten years since the dotcom and telecom meltdown, more than 90 percent of their shareholders' equity was washed away persistently, yet they had the audacity to pay bonuses to their bosses. Such is the anomaly of the corporate world in the twentieth and twenty-first centuries, when inefficiency, indecision, ineffectiveness, indifference, wrong decisions, disastrous corporate results, and the antithesis of shareholders' interests are lavishly rewarded with remunerations and benefits in kind for the bosses.

Many small investors are under the impression that these giant elephants, whether in telecom or non-telecom sectors, are unlikely to drop dead. By their sheer size, they are likely to survive many crashes and shocks on the stock markets. This may well be true. But the survival of corporations that command budgets as large as the state budgets of several African countries does not guarantee that small or minority shareholders will survive the continuous and persistent erosion of their investment values. Small investors are not only likely to lose dividends if performance is negative, but they are most likely to lose their capital altogether. In small and hardly readable print, directors absolve themselves of responsibility by issuing a warning of risk that the values of shares may go up or fall and that the investor may not get back the amount invested. Under the widespread abuse in the corporate world, the warning is likely to be understood as the investors not getting back the amount invested for the simple reason that the fat cats will keep on milking the benefit of their positions, whether their companies are profit makers or loss leaders. If there is no profit to cover the loot of the fat cats, then shareholders have to foot the cost of the luxury of directors' remuneration from their capital. That is why shareholders' equity witnesses a persistent decline under present-day corporate mismanagement.

The furor over Northern Rock Building Society on September 14, 2007, in the financial market is worth a mention. Within a day, this building society lost a third of its share value, and within two working days, it lost 50 percent of it on the stock market. On the third day, the panic of the depositors to withdraw their savings subsided as the Bank of England reassured worried savers that it would provide emergency funds and the FSA reassured people that the building society was solvent. This was considered to be the worst financial crisis to have hit a building society in Britain in almost one and a half centuries. As a result, the values of shares of all building societies were adversely affected. This shows how sensitive stock market prices are to negative development in the market.

There are volumes of lessons to be learned from the market meltdown of the twenty-first century. Perfect competition and rational behavior do not exist in practice; they exist only in textbooks. George Soros contends that these theories and paradigms are false. The uncertainty, bias, incomplete knowledge, irrational or instinctive behavior, guesswork, and other misconceptions of the stock markets lead to faulty decisions.[206]

Soros introduces himself in his book as the son of a Jewish father who had to forge his identity to escape Nazi persecution. He boasts that he has been successful in derivatives trading and hedge funds for the past fifty years, which brought him into contact with top government officials and heads of state. The guru of hedge funds with vast experience reached the conclusion that neither regulations nor macro- or microeconomic theories support the premise that investors and financial markets operate on reliable knowledge. There is a wide gap between thinking and reality because the human brain cannot possibly digest all the available information,[207] not to mention information that is unavailable or concealed intentionally or unintentionally. He cites an example of successful manipulation based on misinformation and blatant lies, like the one promoted by the Bush administration in the name of fighting terrorism to justify invasion of Iraq.[208] He writes, "Politics is more concerned with the pursuit of power than the pursuit of truth."[209]

In politics, as in markets, misinformation, misconceptions, and misinterpretations, that include high-risk derivatives and hedge funds, are rampant. The experts

206 Soros, 5–8.

207 Ibid., 26.

208 Ibid., 38, 43.

209 Ibid., 45.

know the ins and outs of high-risk investment instruments. It is worth comparing and contrasting the views of Soros with those of Muhammad Hashim Kamali on the subject of derivatives. Kamali comes up in favor of futures and options trading as a price stabilizer of essential commodities. Soros distinguishes between acting in one's best interest and acting in the perception of one's best interest.[210] He refutes the equilibrium theory of supply and demand and price stabilization. Imperfection, which characterizes the market, cannot lead to perfection.

In theory, there is a distinction between a hedger and a speculator. The latter enters the futures market to make a quick kill, whereas the former uses futures contracts as insurance policies. A hedger seeks to offset potential losses to protect the underlying asset value.[211]

If one studies the variables that affect the market and all those that operate in the market, the perception of investors may misguide him or her into believing that stockbrokers or traders or financial advisors are acting in investors' best interest, which may not be true. Many investors who blindly rely on others' recommendations may find themselves cheated simply because their best interests never matched the brokers' best interests in the first place. Similarly, the cartels or major players who control the financial markets may find themselves in a position where their business interests dictate that investors are given spurious and misleading projected figures of performance. Later on, when the investors discover, at their peril, the reality, stock traders or brokers can always take refuge in the excuse that after all, the figures of performance were only projected and not actual and were based on expectations. If they speak the truth, they lose customers. Thus, if the worst of the worst investment funds and phony schemes attract interest from some naïve investors, this is possible only when the promoters, intermediaries, or fund managers have successfully concealed some key facts about the dubious funds they promote.

Shares are issued at a high premium over their nominal values, such as shares of one pence nominal value offered for ten pounds each. This is done in expectation of a future growth in profit, which may never be realized. Yet companies may get away with issuing shares at phenomenal premiums by misrepresenting their past-performance figures. From a cautious investor's viewpoint, there is no alternative to studying

---

210 Ibid., 57.

211 Mitchell, 7.

the past five years' audited accounts to assess whether the companies promoting the shares or their management have proven their worth or are hiding their worthlessness behind small print and legal jargon prepared by their lawyers. When the true scale of abuse in the financial and stock markets is unveiled, it might make small scandals in politics look like no event.

CHAPTER 9

THE ROLE OF DERIVATIVES AND FUTURES AND OPTIONS TRADING

Kennedy Mitchell writes, "Stock futures, by their nature of being a derivative and agreement for a future transaction, can be purchased or sold as an opening transaction. The principal [*sic*] that a buyer exists for every seller and vice versa in the futures market allows the ability to sell futures contract...If you believe that a particular stock's price will decline from current prices, you can sell a single stock futures contract to an individual who believes the opposite."[212]

Professor Susan Strange[213] assesses succinctly the Western financial system and compares it to a "vast casino." She writes, "Instead of roulette, blackjack, or poker, there is a dealing to be done—the foreign exchange market and all its variations or in bonds, government securities or shares. In all these markets you may place bets on the future."[214] Futures and options play a pivotal role in causing violent swings in the stock market. The futures market allows speculators to enter into futures contracts to buy or sell currencies, commodities, financial instruments, and indices[215] at a predetermined date in future. The full price of the contract is payable on maturity date. A performance bond is required from the buyer.[216] For a small outlay—normally a certain percentage of the contract value—a hedger can offset risk of investment in one asset against another.[217] If the underlying assets increase in value, the futures contract

212 Mitchell, 58.

213 Professor of International Political Economy at the University of Warwick and emeritus and professor at the London School of Economics.

214 Strange, 1.

215 The indicators of stock market performance.

216 Johnson, 139.

217 Jacobs, 341.

value also increases, and vice versa. Arbitrage trading is based on currently prevailing price differences for the same assets in different markets.

In Britain, options are traded on the London International Financial Futures Exchange (LIFFE). In America, the Chicago Board Options Exchange is the third largest in the United States. There is a high probability that an investor might lose on futures just as the punter loses on bets. Foreign exchange contracts are traded on organized exchanges to exchange two or more currencies at a future date. The purchaser agrees to purchase, and the seller agrees to sell specified currencies on specified dates.

A further innovation in this field is options trading; there are two kinds. A "call" option confers the right, but not the obligation, to buy a quantity of commodity, currency, stock indices, or financial instruments at a specified price at any time up to a fixed future date. By contrast, a "put" option confers the right, but not the obligation, to sell a quantity of commodity, currency, stock indices, or financial instruments at a specified price before a fixed future date.[218] The buyer of a call option will not exercise this option until the market price is more than the strike price.[219] If the market price is less than the strike price, he or she allows the option to expire because he or she is better off buying the asset in the market.

The buyer of a call option protects himself or herself against rising prices, and the buyer of a put option protects himself or herself against falling prices. The buyers of both options pay sellers a premium for undertaking such risks.[220] If the prices do not move according to the expectation of the buyer, then he or she loses the premium but gains the full market value of the asset.[221] The writer of the option—the seller—takes the risk that in the case of a call option, prices will not rise, and that in the case of a put option, prices will not fall. The strike or exercise price is the price at which the buyer of a call or put option has the right to buy or sell his or her futures contract.[222]

The buyer has a right to go long—to buy in case of a call option—or to go short—to sell in case of a put option. A European-style option can be exercised on the expiration date only, whereas an American-style option can be exercised up to and including

218 Morris, 159, and Johnson, 141.

219 Johnson, 145.

220 Jacobs, 20–21.

221 Ibid., 49–50.

222 Ibid., 346.

the expiration date. Traded options become worthless if they are not exercised by the expiration dates. The price of a traded option is made up of its intrinsic value—the market price minus the exercise price. A premium over intrinsic value is called "time value." The options that have intrinsic value are called "in the money" options—when profit does appear on the futures contract.

The in-the-money options show profit in two ways:

1. In case of call, when the price of an asset is more than the strike price
2. In case of put, when the price of an asset is less than the strike price

Thus, if the market value of an asset exceeds the exercise price, the owner of a call option acquires the asset at the strike price and sells it in the market at a higher price. Similarly, if the market value of an asset is less than the exercise price, the owner of a put option sells the asset at the strike price and buys it in the market at a lower price.

The option is out of money if it has no intrinsic value and if the future price is above the strike price, in which case exercising the option would result in a loss. The out-of-money option shows loss in two ways:

1. In case of call, when the price of an asset is lower than the strike price
2. In case of put, when the price of an asset is more than the strike price

When the strike price and the market price are identical, the option is said to be "at the money."[223] In this case, the owner of the call option is indifferent regarding whether to exercise the option or buy the asset on the market.

These derivative products are ultra risky investments. Yet by the end of March 1995, the total outstanding value of derivatives was $55.7 trillion, and this amount swelled to about $100 trillion by the end of 1997.[224] In the United States alone, in 1998, investors held $800 billion of share options.[225] An investment manager gave his own explanation to Jonathan Davis about derivatives. He believes that if the decision of the

223 Johnson, 337–44.

224 Warburton, 113.

225 Ibid., 199.

fund managers is 100 percent right, then they are cheating.[226] With regard to derivatives, he believes they are "an expensive broker's toy." When he was asked whether investment was an art or a science, he replied, "it's trial and error."[227]

In the summer of 1998, global stock markets faced extreme volatility in the wake of the collapse of the Russian economy and bond market.[228] The Black-Scholes option pricing theory, named after the Nobel Prize winner in economic sciences in 1997, initiated the trading in derivatives on organized exchanges and OTC schemes.[229]

Equity derivatives were meant to reduce risk in falling markets.[230] However, investor behavior is prone to create a trend in the same direction—to sell when the market falls and to buy when it rises. By contrast, the sellers of portfolio insurance seek to "buy low and sell high."[231] The volatility in the stock market makes hedging very expensive. Premiums have to be renewed for stock-index options every three to six months in a falling market.[232] Therefore, few institutional investors can afford it. There may be no escape but to take huge losses.

In the 1980s, the US stock exchanges saw a boom in options trading; it was possible to place a bet on any commodity, and it would either rise or fall within a given period of time.[233] These option funds are registered in one of the so-called tax havens or unregulated financial centers, such as the Cayman Islands, the Cook Islands, and Liechtenstein. Liechtenstein has more registered limited companies than citizens! The fund managers can then employ with liberty their gambling spree while maintaining the physical presence of management at home. Hence, the board of directors of funds registered in offshore centers can operate from the United Kingdom but outside the ambit of the UK Companies Acts and regulations. The authorities are prone to turn a blind eye under the pretext that the funds are registered outside their jurisdiction.

---

226 Davis, 152.

227 Ibid., 154.

228 Jacobs, 1.

229 Ibid., 3.

230 Ibid., 4, 16.

231 Ibid., 61, 65.

232 Deborah Hargreaves, "Companies and Markets: Swinging Times Make Mark on Cost of Hedging," *Financial Times*, October 14, 2002.

233 Strange, 53.

Options become very complex and risky when dealers try to hedge simultaneously the interest rate, cost of finance, and exchange rates in different currencies.[234] A lone trader, Nick Leeson, brought down the two-hundred-year-old Barings Bank in 1995 by losing $1.3 billion in futures and options. Daiwa Bank in New York was brought down because of a loss of $1.1 billion by a single trader.[235] In 1993, the German giant Metallgesellschaft lost $1.3 billion on oil futures. In 1994, Procter & Gamble lost $157 million on swaps contracts.[236] In the same year, Orange County in California faced bankruptcy due to swap-deal losses in interest rates. The list of abuses is inexhaustible.

John Rusnak contributed to a series of frauds in currency futures trade. On October 24, 2002, Reuters News Agency reported that he was involved in a $692.1 million fraud involving Allied Irish Bank. Rusnak was employed by the bank's US subsidiary, Allfirst Financial Inc. The prosecution alleged that Rusnak was a rogue trader. The case attracted public interest because it was one of the biggest banking scandals in the United States. Allied Irish Bank was blamed for weak internal controls. Rusnak's style resembled Leeson's style. As the yen was recording more and more falls, Rusnak kept buying more and more yen. Having convinced his bosses that he was gaining in the currency market, his gambling instincts gave him further incentive to capitalize on his bosses' wait-and-see attitude. In addition to a salary of $110,000, he was to be paid a handsome bonus of $220,000, calculated on concocted figures.[237]

Negligence of senior management opens a door for overambitious traders to become rogues. Otherwise, it is not possible for a lone trader to authorize deals worth millions, without internal checks and internal controls being in operation at each stage of decision making. But as William Leith rightly comments, "Bank executives, often men in their fifties and sixties, are people who grew up in the markets of the 1970s and 1980s...They are dinosaurs."[238] As more and more people entrust their savings and investments to banks and financial institutions, the sheer increase in the inflow of funds provides a temptation to take unwarranted risks. Leith comments that a decade ago, the volume of global foreign exchange deals used to be

234 Jacobs, 248.

235 Ibid., 255.

236 Swap contracts are entered "to exchange assets or a series of cash flows for a specified period...at predetermined intervals" (Johnson, 149).

237 William Leith, "How to Lose a Billion," *Guardian*, October 26, 2002.

238 Ibid.

$50 billion to $60 billion a day. By 1997, they were a staggering $15 trillion a day. He further sheds light on similar cases of rogue trading. Iguchi at the Manhattan branch of Daiwa Bank lost in the bond market from 1984 to 1995 and continued until he could go no further.

Peter Young, the head of Morgan Grenfell's European Growth Unit Trust, bought shares in Solv-Ex. This US Corporation had come up with a fanciful idea of extracting black gold from sand; it was an opportunity of a generation, not to be missed. In 1996, although Solv-Ex was under investigation, Young went ahead in committing $400 million of unit trust holders' funds, which, in the misguided perception of uninformed investors, was a relatively safe investment.

Because futures and options trading is very complex, banks' "dinosaurs" are reluctant to expose their lack of understanding and knowledge about the complications involved. If the gambling spree of a lone futures and options trader goes undetected for several years, this could have serious implications. This might imply that senior management and internal and external auditors are negligent.

The falls of the Japanese market in the 1990s were also due to Nikkei put warrants.[239] The notional value of all OTC derivatives worldwide was estimated at more than $47 trillion in 1995.[240] Out of all derivatives, warrants carry hyper risk. They give the holder a right to subscribe in shares at a fixed price at a predetermined future date.[241] They do not carry any voting rights and do not entitle the holder to dividends. If the holder decides not to subscribe in shares, then the warrants become worthless.[242]

Frank Partnoy's book *FIASCO: Blood in the Water on Wall Street* is a self-confession of a derivatives trader employed by one of the most reputable investment banks on Wall Street. It portrays the obscene scenario in derivatives trading, whereby clients are trapped with false ratings of bond issues, and the accounting rules are bent and manipulated to conceal the risk involved. At the time of issue of junk bonds and other high-risk derivatives, salespeople are absolutely aware not only that the bonds are

239 Jacobs, 255–57.

240 Ibid., 262.

241 Chapman, 44.

242 Samuels and Wilkes, 90.

going to default on the guaranteed interest payment but that they will not honor repayment of the guaranteed principal, either. If the scheme goes bust, all the guarantees go down the drain too.

Many institutional investors are tempted to commit their funds by supplying bosses with escorts—men or women—and extravagant sprees of gambling and all-night disco parties in the red-light district of Manhattan, with free dining, dancing, and drinks—all at the cost of investors or members of the public who have trusted the Mafia in the world of finance with their pension and insurance money and investment portfolios. The cost that is preloaded on the issue of bonds is not only that of millions of dollars of fees and commissions for investment bankers and traders but also that of the loot disguised as entertainment of clients.

Neither the mutual fund managers, who are eager to throw away or dump their clients' money, nor the investment bankers behind the issue of multi-collateralized derivatives are trustworthy. The only concern of investment bankers is to make sure that they get their fees of millions of dollars, and the only worry of traders and brokers is to hit the million mark in commissions. When halfway through it transpires that investors have lost all of their capital, the promoters of bonds get restless and worried to death that their commissions will not be paid in full!

Every time an investment scheme that is the brainchild of the most sophisticated and criminally minded investment bankers goes bust, a nail is hammered in the coffin of capitalism, and public confidence in capitalism is shaken. When high-risk derivatives, which find their place even on the balance sheets of reputable blue-chip companies, go bust, investors face damaging repercussions. As investors suffer from insomnia, in political circles there is not a whisper calling for a trial against the promoters because politicians have benefited directly—if not from entertainment in the red-light district of Manhattan and Chinatown, then from political donations. These eventually pass into trusts for their children and grandchildren, registered in unregulated offshore financial centers.

Even the most reputable financial centers in the world suffer from the bug of corruption. The promoters of derivatives employ trickery or outright bribery for pushing the issue of bonds or shares and stocks. Gifts of wine and tickets for cricket or hockey matches are used merely as tips for winning the loyalty of influential clients. When it comes to aggressive selling techniques, they have at their disposal the whole industry, which trades in human misery. Worse still, when it comes to promoting bonds and stocks connected with raising finances for procurement of arms and weapons, Arab sheikhs, with prayer beads in their hands, are exposed to the sin industry and are induced to offload their country's resources in bonds for buying arms and ammunition, which they and their succeeding generations are never likely to need, except in fulfilling the dire needs of terrorist groups. International media in general, and Arabic media in particular, have widely reported in their news bulletins and comments the names of certain countries, one of them a member of NATO and others oil-producing countries of the Middle East, as having provided arms, finances, logistics, safe transit, and support to terrorists from eighty countries who are threatening the safety and security of the United States and European countries, as happened in the mayhem caused in Paris and Brussels, having already destroyed at least three countries in the Middle East. All this is happening under the nose of the international community and the United Nations, with the free flowing of funds permitted under the international banking system.

Misleading tactics in investment banking are employed because these schemes do not provide even a meager productive economic service. The only service they render is to fill the pockets of investment bankers, their brokers, and corrupt government officials at the cost of misery to investors and innocent members of the public. They remain unconcerned with the social disservice to individuals, communities, and the economy of their own nations.

None of the dubious investment schemes, either in the form of high-interest-paying bonds (which end up being paid from capital) or other junky derivatives, stand a flicker of a chance of acceptance if they do not carry the name of a reputable investment bank. Unfortunately, investors are not literate enough to thwart the deceptive selling tactics of the rogue traders. Otherwise, investors could stop the life-support machine of derivative traders by deciding not to invest, no matter how attractive the window dressing is.

The filth and obscenity portrayed in Partnoy's book regarding the character, conduct, and language of derivatives traders on Wall Street compels one to contrast those traders' services to those of sewage cleaners in the overflowing gutters in the ghettos of Mumbai. The latter relieve people of misery and desperation by undertaking a useful economic activity, whereas the former cause misery to people and their families by gambling with the money entrusted to them and destroying the economy of the country for their selfish interest. In the process, the system itself provides them with the platform, mechanism, and necessary legal cover to undertake their disservice to the nation and its people in favor of the rich and powerful elites and politicians. This is the grim reality of the present-day capitalist system, which is filled to the brim with hypocrisy and betrayal.

The conclusion one can safely reach by studying Partnoy's book is that the entire training program of salespeople and their managers in the investment industry is geared toward hunting for gullible members of the public, taking undue advantage of their naïveté, and literally ripping them off of their lifetime savings. This means that thousands of savers might have to spend the rest of their lives on state benefits, which, in all probability, may not even cover the cost of the basic necessities of life. Thus, under legally articulated manipulation, lawyers are employed at colossal fees to find loopholes in the law. Their motive is to dig out exceptions to the rules for investment banks and their traders and save them for playing roulette with the law of the country. As the fees charged by investment bankers and fund managers tend to skyrocket the riskier the venture, little do they care when floating derivatives that either the borrowing banks or the borrowing governments might default. When they do default, the intermediaries have safely pocketed their fees, leaving investors in agony and limbo.

The financial and economic system in some countries is corrupt to the core. Before borrowing millions on reputable stock exchanges, officials are dead sure that they will not be able to honor their obligations. But this is the safest channel available to corrupt government officials to help themselves to the money, which will eventually have to be repaid by their own public. Bribery is repackaged under several different names. It is taken in the name of a "facility," "gift," or "donation." And the officials in the borrowing countries legitimize bribe taking, provided it is not called a "bribe."

CHAPTER 10

THE ROLE OF SPECULATORS

As far back as 1855, H. von Mongolds cautioned on profit and speculation in the stock markets. He said the likelihood of losing money exceeded the likelihood of gaining because the markets "by their specialized nature are essentially speculative."[243]

Professor Strange explains the essence of normal supply and demand, which causes movement of prices, compared to speculation, which vitiates prices violently. She writes, "A speculative market can be defined as one in which prices move in response to the balance of opinion regarding the future movement of prices," which in itself is dictated by uncertainty. She continues: "A speculative market most resembles a racecourse, where there is a market for bets on the horses (or dogs) that will win or get a place."[244]

It was margin dealing that encouraged the boom of the 1920s, which ended in the meltdown of 1929 on Wall Street. In 1896, H. C. Emery observed that speculators heavily depend "on chance for their success...The evil is further increased by the margin system."[245] With financial markets working around the clock, short-term speculation in futures and options increased enormously because only a small margin of outlay was needed to place a bet. Due to the resulting volatility of the financial markets, fund managers were prone to use long-term assets for short-term quick gains.[246] This attitude of the fund managers almost nullified the long-term strategy in the stock market. The only long-term phenomenon might be two or three violent jolts that the stock market was likely to suffer in a decade, thus wiping out most of the capital gains.

243 Strange, iiv.

244 Ibid., 111.

245 Ibid., 112.

246 Ibid., 114–15.

The disastrous consequences of falls of the stock market are due to excessive credits, where speculators are tempted to buy stocks for which they do not have money to pay, and they are tempted to sell stocks that are not in their possession. Speculation does not create wealth. It allocates wealth poorly.

Michael Walters, a columnist with the *Daily Mail* with thirty-six years' experience, wrote that the stock market "does dance to the tune played by the big money," which has the ultimate say.[247] He observed that prior to the 1987 crash, "Millions of small investors were coming to gamble for the first time." They were motivated by the 1986 Big Bang, which brought drastic changes to the market operation. With the touch of a button, contact was established between dealers and investors on a global scale.[248] The author described the reality of the stock market, which small investors often miss: "Sure as night follows day, stock market slump follows stock market boom... The slump is followed by a boom."[249] Walters further stressed that there is nothing called responsible investment,[250] in view of the fact that even "giant companies can be dominated by crooks," such as media tycoon Maxwell and Polly Peck.[251] Conrad Black, a Canadian-born member of the House of Lords in the United Kingdom, found guilty by a jury in Chicago for embezzling £60 million of shareholders' money, was not the last crook.[252] Like Robert Maxwell, he was a hedonist with never-ending greed at the expense of others.

Professor Strange writes, "If the uncertainty over exchange rates and interest rates and over general economic prospects continues, the tendency to gambling and speculation, to chasing the fast buck by fair means or foul, is going to persist too."[253] This scenario is prevailing as well in the new century as it did in the old.

Share dealing is controlled by market makers, who buy shares in bulk and set buying and selling price limits. Investors have to operate within those limits.[254] When the computer screens show that the price of a particular share has fallen, outsiders may

---

247 Walters, 8.

248 Ibid., 9–10.

249 Ibid., 11.

250 Ibid., 32.

251 Ibid., 33.

252 Reuters, July 13, 2007, http://today.reuters.com/news/.

253 Strange, 173.

254 Chapman, 37–38.

get the impression that some changes have occurred or the company has produced financial results. This may not be the case. Market makers might be competing with each other by lowering the price simply to attract buyers. This may sound unfair. But as Walters wrote, "No one ever said the city had to be fair."[255] This explains why certain shares shoot up in a spectacular way and suddenly go out of favor. So one may ask, What about the city code of conduct and other rules? Walter explains, "Self-interest is the only rule which is honored consistently."[256]

If the market makers want to sell shares they do not hold, they raise the price to tempt others who do hold these shares to sell them on the market so that the market makers can buy them. This means that the market makers may buy at higher price just to fulfill their contractual obligation. But in the process, they may maneuver the psychology of other holders. Instead of buying the shortfall quantity at a higher price, they might even knock down the price and create a panic in the market, forcing other shareholders to sell.[257] As a result, they may suffer a momentary loss to gain overall.

It is stockbrokers, not small investors, who have information about the game being played behind the screens. For example, when a company announces healthy financial results, its shares start to fall as an initial reaction. City commentators comment that the results are not according to market expectation. Small investors might panic and dispose of their holdings. After several days, the same shares start to rise. The phrase "market expectation" ought to be understood as "market maker's expectation." Mark Mobius, who had a knack with the emerging markets of the Far East, testified that an investor in the Thailand Stock Exchange held a gun to his head and threatened to kill himself if the market maker did not make the stock market rise.[258]

Speculators have a number of tools at their disposal. "Stagging" is the term used for the purchase of shares in new issues, with the purpose of selling them at a profit on the commencement of dealings. Walters noted, "It is a gambling bonanza that leaves Vegas standing."[259] As soon as the dealing starts, the players could pocket millions of pounds.

---

255 Walters, 68.

256 Ibid., 69.

257 Ibid., 70.

258 Davis, 185–87.

259 Walters, 116–17.

Sometimes the market is manipulated by speculators who issue exaggerated statements to the press on the prospect of certain shares. This is meant to give a boost to these shares.[260] Based on his longstanding experience in tipping shares, Walters advises investors that because "stock market money is gambling money," they should invest only what they can afford to lose. Then they can play the market either aggressively or safely.[261] He advises that speculative investors who are in the game for a quick kill should be on the lookout for companies likely to attract takeover bids. Normally, companies in the growth industry with a good track record of past performance and a strong asset base attract bids. He warns, though, that speculators are experts in spreading rumors.[262] There are simply too many conmen out there. So share pushers who have no stake in the company are to be avoided.[263] There is a thin line of demarcation between takeover activities and speculation. Executives favor takeovers and mergers because if successful, they can draw massive salaries, bonuses, and share options that are then borne by the shareholders.[264]

Speculation is based not on rationality but on conjecture. Biotech shares, in the absence of any scientific breakthroughs, rarely show profit. Yet they were booming in 1995. By 1998, they had fallen from grace.[265] High-tech shares were skyrocketing in 1998. But after the mid-2000s, they declined to the level that they became penny shares by 2002.

The manipulative power that speculators wield can play havoc with the shares of major companies. The FSA launched an inquiry into the claim that speculators had spread false rumors against HBOS, which triggered sharp falls in its share price on March 19, 2008. The *Daily Telegraph* reported that a hedge fund was set up by what it called a "dirty tricks unit" to affect share prices. HBOS is a major company that provides financial products, with the Bank of Scotland being part of its group and millions of shareholders on its register. A mere rumor by speculators for making personal gains can ruin the interest of millions of small shareholders.

---

260 Ibid., 152–53.

261 Ibid., 168–69.

262 Ibid., 202–4, 206.

263 Ibid., 216–17.

264 Engler, 73.

265 Ibid., 183.

An inquiry into the mood of stock traders adds an additional factor in the jigsaw of market maneuvers. In his study published in the *Proceedings of the National Academy of Sciences* on April 15, 2008, John Coates, a research fellow at Cambridge University, disclosed that upheavals in the stock market are like those caused in the body of a person who is taking steroids like testosterone. This influences the behavior of stock traders on the floor of the market. Its level in the blood rises with competition. As the trader wins, testosterone increases, and as he loses, it decreases. In the former case, he is prone to taking big risks. When the level of steroids increases in animals, they become aggressive. Similarly, when stock traders experience it, they take risks at dangerous levels. This discovery has added a new paradigm in the moody upheavals of the stock market. In the morning, if testosterone is high in the blood of stock traders, they are likely to end up with big profits. If it keeps on rising in their blood, the traders are likely to take irresponsible decisions and high risks.

CHAPTER 11

FACTORS FOR INVESTORS TO CONSIDER

A serious investor, in contrast to a speculator, considers important market ratios, such as price-earnings ratio, earnings per share, and net asset value per share, over a period of three to five years. The lower the P/E ratio, the more attractive the stock is. In addition, reliability of fixed assets—the gearing of borrowing in relation to shareholders' equity—is also considered. Company results and directors' reports are studied to find out whether the company is facing any litigation or a significant shift in the demand for its products. If the investor is more interested in income than capital growth, then dividend yield is considered.

Dividend yield is the value of a company's annual dividend in percentage terms of the current share price. Return on capital is stated in terms of capital invested, called "shareholders' equity." Net worth of the company is net assets—total assets less liabilities. This is also called "shareholders' funds." The PEG factor is considered in investment decisions. PEG is the ratio of the expected growth rate to the P/E ratio, based on projected figures, not historic figures.

The most important useful source of information an investor can rely on is a company's published accounts. Yet an unqualified audit report is not a guarantee that the company's operations are financially sound. The criminally fraudulent Robert Maxwell's companies and Bank of Credit and Commerce International (BCCI) got away with clean audit reports from renowned audit firms over a number of years. It is prudent for small investors to concentrate on cash flow. If it is positive after paying dividends and capital expenses, then the next step is to compare incoming cash from operations with operating profits. If there is a disparity between the two, then the investor should investigate the figures further.[266]

266 Walters, 224.

Companies may go on reporting increases in sales and profits. But if they fail to provide for asset replacement in real terms, after adjusting for inflation, then their shares cannot sustain growth. The statements of the company's chairman and managing director about the future prospects of their company have to be taken with a grain of salt. At times, the prospect statements are full of exaggerations. Even if the company is on the verge of liquidation, directors are prone to reassure shareholders of the bright future and prosperity waiting just around the corner. Many shareholders do not bother to study the figures. Even if they glance at them, they are not likely to find their way through the jungle of figures, which are too complicated for the average layperson to understand.

Professor Haugen suggests that if any expert claims that there is a mountain of evidence supporting his hypothesis, then it should be known that the mountain is quickly eroding.[267] He further claims that the market commits big errors in pricing stocks, and it cannot see through the cobweb of figures in the accounts. However, there is a growing tendency in the market to disregard reported figures.

Haugen proposes certain criteria for assessing what he calls "measures of cheapness" ratios, which include the following:

1. Earnings-to-price ratio
2. Earnings-to-price trend
3. Book-to-price ratio
4. Book-to-price trend
5. Dividend-to-price ratio
6. Dividend-to-price trend
7. Cash-flow-to-price ratio
8. Cash-flow-to-price trend
9. Sales-to-price ratio
10. Sales-to-price trend, where price is the current market price and trend stands for the five-year monthly figures.[268]

267 Haugen, 2.

268 Ibid., 46.

He also proposes certain "measures of profitability" ratios, which include the following:

1. Profit margin
2. Profit margin trend
3. Capital turnover
4. Capital-turnover trend
5. Return on assets
6. Return-on-assets trend
7. Return on equity
8. Return-on-equity trend
9. Earnings growth

Earnings-growth surprise, where growth is calculated by comparing actual earnings with average earnings over a period of five years and surprise is calculated by comparing the difference between reported earnings and projected earnings.[269]

Added to this jigsaw of ratios are other factors that are employed to predict what is highly unpredictable i.e. corporate performance, which is affected by representation or misrepresentation of facts.

Haugen gives a profile of "big, liquid, financially sound, low-risk momentum in the market, profitable in every dimension, and becoming more profitable in every way" and selling at the cheapest possible price in the market. He calls this a "dream profile."[270] It does not exist, and it will never exist in reality, but it exists when investors start to daydream and build palaces in the air. If brokers or stock dealers sense that their clients are in a state of slumber or wishful thinking, then they may grasp the opportunity to take their clients for a ride.

If there is a clash of interest between the stockbroker or stock dealer and the investor, then the latter is likely to be used as a sacrificial ram. If investment advisors have not signed any declaration of intent or investment advisory agreement (a scenario that widely prevailed prior to the Financial Services Act 1986 in the United Kingdom), then they enjoy a relaxed atmosphere to manipulate and misappropriate

269 Ibid., 47.

270 Ibid., 82.

the funds of naïve investors who have trusted them and their judgment. In a way, the Financial Services Act 1986, repealed by the Financial Services and Markets Act 2000, introduced some controls over the widely prevailing abuses in the United Kingdom. But as legislators became vigilant, abusers discovered new methods and means to con the vulnerable investors. The abuse continues unabated.

CHAPTER 12

INSIDER INFORMATION

Walters warns that *insider trading*, which is the use of privileged information by management, is a daily occurrence. Although illegal, he says, "it is impossible to stop and extremely difficult to prove." When brokers buy a large block of shares at a wholesale price and execute client orders from the shares they hold, conflict of interest is the norm.[271]

The Role of Charts

Speculators increasingly tend to rely on charts. A *chart* is a graphical representation of prices over a period of time. Chartists establish a trend of investor interest in the share, on the basis of market price. They disregard economic fundamentals and operational results of the company.[272] On the basis of uptrend and downtrend, trade cycles in the commodities market are established.[273] A pattern may take several years to form. The power of computer software is used to equip the speculator with the ability to forecast price movements. Complex analytical and statistical tools, such as regression analysis, relative strength, and moving averages, are used in the process.[274] Because investors are subject to "herd instinct," this is what chartists do—they follow the crowd and show their behavior on graphs.[275]

---

271 Walters, 95–96

272 Stewart, xiii–xiv.

273 Ibid., 8.

274 Ibid., 87–93.

275 Ibid., 102.

This is easier said than done. The speculator wants to know when it is just about the right time to get into the market and when it is just about the right time to get out. But "the right time" depends on individual judgment. If chartists believe that when companies are reporting profits, it is the right time to sell, they run the risk of getting out of the game too soon. If they believe that when companies are reporting losses, it is the right time to buy, then they may be taking a deep dive. This could prove to be a recipe for disaster because company shares may not recover. At times, "mathematical sophistry" is employed to conceal the truth.[276]

Chartists concentrate on market peaks and troughs. They predict high and low points, as well as the time to buy and the time to sell.[277] One more factor is emphasized in charting—"the importance of symmetry...between time and distance."[278] This is applicable whether a person is a long-term investor or a speculator, although the time lag differs between the two. The former buys a share and holds it through thick and thin. The latter commits his or her or other people's money with a view of making a quick profit.[279] The difference between the two should be clear. "There is an element of the casino in speculation...There is an element of luck in long-term investment."[280]

Despite all the precautions and analytical methods employed by chartists, there are no "hard and fast rules" for "cutting losses and taking profits."[281] Had there been such rules, then the crashes of 1929 and 1987 and the recurrence of recession would have been foreseen. Some analysts consider charting to be a "dangerous nonsense."[282]

Billionaire George Soros, a world-famous speculator, remarks, "Unexpected and chaotic movements of financial markets might destroy society."[283] Therefore, if speculation breeds on greed, some ways have to be found whereby, in the words of Milton Friedman, "greed will do the least harm."[284] Maynard Keynes is reported to have said, "The game of professional investment is intolerably boring and exacting to anyone

276 Heller, 22.

277 Chapman, 159–60.

278 Stewart, 103.

279 Ibid., 115.

280 Ibid., 116.

281 Ibid., 157.

282 Davis, 33.

283 Chapman, 96.

284 Ibid., 142.

who is entirely exempt from the gambling instinct."[285] During the European Monetary Union (ERM) crisis in September 1992, George Soros quite legally brought the sterling to its knees. In the process, he walked away with $1 billion in profit. The currency that becomes prey to the designs of speculators may have to be devalued—if not officially, then in the international money market.

Ultra speculative instruments like savings and loans (S&L) have left the most damaging effect on the financial world. When they were deregulated in the Reagan era, competition increased as companies aimed to obtain federally insured deposits. Thrifts fell into the hands of organized criminals. Money lent by financial houses moved to and fro between clients and associated companies of brokers. "If loans went bad, nobody would lose—except taxpayers."[286] At each transfer, the book value of the collateral asset was artificially inflated, and fees and commission were charged. In one case, a property worth $2 million reached, in the process, $175 million. "Speculators bought sumptuous mansions, luxury yachts, and bought politicians from both the parties."[287]

By 1987, the scheme had collapsed, leaving seventeen hundred S&Ls bankrupt. Their failures left the Justice Department with twenty-one thousand criminal referrals by 1990. Charles Keating, who had played the game within the legal framework, pocketed from S&Ls in California a salary package of $41.5 million for himself and his family. Engler writes that Keating, who became an advisor to President George W. Bush, employed Alan Greenspan as a consultant and developed a friendship with attorney general Edwin Meese. When the senior Bush administration tried to regulate S&Ls, it ended up with overvalued properties, some of which were toxic-waste sites. Consequently, the collapse of Keating's S&Ls landed US taxpayers with a bill of $2.5 billion.[288]

Money Laundering and Financial Crimes

The last decade of the twentieth century was dominated by banking scandals. In July 1991, regulators led by the Bank of England closed down BCCI and its network of branches in seventy countries. Out of $14 billion worth of assets, $12.4 billion had

285 Davis, 113.

286 Engler, 115.

287 Ibid., 116.

288 Ibid., 117.

disappeared. The bank had lost heavily on speculative trade in derivatives. To conceal its losses, it created fictitious debts.[289] The scandal threatened the collapse of central banks in several third-world countries.

BCCI was implicated for money laundering and handling the funds of terrorists, drug barons, and rogues among arms producers and dealers. The press widely reported that the Bank of England knew about the activities of BCCI long before taking any action. On February 5, 2001, the *Senate Money Laundering Report* named US banks for lack of care in allowing themselves to be used "to launder hundreds of millions of dollars, obtained through drug trafficking, financial fraud, and bribery." The report stressed that the abuse was widespread and continuous. It expressed grave concern that all the banks that were investigated maintained accounts with offshore banks. They had connections with shell banks, with no existence in any jurisdiction. The report accused the US banks of gross negligence and charged that Internet gambling monies were transferred on behalf of foreign banks they had never heard of.

The report continued that these banks helped their foreign correspondents conduct "high-yield investment scams" and induced investors to transfer funds. The banks then refused to return the monies to investors, who were defrauded under shabby investment schemes. Clients were asked to pay "advance fees for loans." The fees were retained, and no loans were given. The report named and shamed household institutions in the American banking system that laundered dirty money.[290]

This was the situation a decade after the closure of BCCI, which was subjected to several elaborate investigatory reports and research studies.[291] A clear affinity was established between BCCI and persons at the center of political establishment in the Middle East and in the United States. But most of them escaped accountability, leaving behind thousands of depositors and creditors to bear the brunt for having been misled and defrauded. In the case of Maxwell too, the research studies portrayed his contacts with high-profile political figures.[292]

289 *Al-Hayat*, issue 11031, April 26, 1993.

290 US Department of State, "Texts: Excerpt of Senate Money Laundering Report, Press Release," http://usinfo.state.gov/topical/global/drugs/01020501.htm, accessed on September 21, 2002.

291 One of the in-depth studies published on BCCI is James Ring Adams and Douglas Frantz, *A Full-Service Bank: How BCCI Stole Billions around the World* (London: Simon & Schuster, 1992).

292 One of the in-depth studies published about the rise and fall of the Maxwell Empire is Tom Bower, *Maxwell: The Final Verdict* (London: HarperCollins Publishers, 1995).

An International Financial Action Task Force Report (1990) on money laundering disclosed that out of "$122 billion per year" revenue from "cocaine, heroin, and cannabis" in the United States and Europe, $85 billion was laundered. Apart from the offshore centers of the Bahamas, Cayman Islands, and Virgin Islands, reputable financial centers in Switzerland and Luxembourg were employed for wiring dirty money.[293] Offshore facilities provide a convenient vehicle for illegal activities such as the following:

1. A person may build up debts at home or in the outside world and, to avoid paying his or her creditors, may smuggle out his money into offshore accounts, where anonymity is guaranteed, so that these funds remain outside the reach of his or her creditors.
2. Because disclosure requirements for company accounts are not stringent in offshore funds, management can easily manipulate company results, showing fictitious profits. For example, after Enron filed for insolvency on December 2, 2001, it was discovered that a series of false accounting had taken place throughout the 1990s involving the company and its auditing company, Arthur Andersen, which was one of the five largest accounting firms in the world. The auditing firm also had to be dissolved. As the scandal was unearthed, Enron's share value fell from $90 to half a dollar.
3. Money laundering takes place through offshore facilities.
4. Unscrupulous stock traders and fund managers find a soft corner for tax evasion in offshore facilities.
5. It is claimed that professional criminal and terrorist activities are financed through offshore accounts.

An analytical paper titled "Financial System Abuse, Financial Crime, and Money Laundering—Background Paper," prepared by the International Monetary Fund (February 12, 2001)[294] makes interesting reading. The paper was prepared to protect the international financial system from abuse, which includes taking and giving bribes

---

293 Melissa Benn, "How to Make Dirty Money Squeaky Clean," *New Internationalist*, issue 224, October 1991.

294 http://imf.org/external/np/ml/2001/eng/021201.pdf.

under different names and trafficking of drug money. Annex III of the paper states that the Financial Crimes Division of the US Secret Service has drawn attention to four areas of abuse:

1. Where fictitious negotiable instruments are produced, with supporting fraudulent documents, "to underline loans or to be sold to individual investors, pension funds, or retirement accounts"
2. Where fictitious checks, bonds, and securities are produced
3. Where advance-fee fraud is committed by an enterprise operating from offshore centers, claiming to represent a foreign government
4. Where accounts are taken over by computer hackers who succeed in accessing Internet accounts through identity fraud

In his speech on February 20, 2007, to an FSA Fraud Advisory Panel Discussion forum, Edna Young, head of Financial Crimes Operations, confessed that fraud is "notoriously difficult to measure." But its damaging repercussions to consumers who lose their lifetime savings and to financial institutions that lose huge amounts cannot be underestimated. He said, "There is also evidence of financial fraud feeding terrorist activity, both in the United Kingdom and internationally."[295]

However, Edna Young's speech provided inspiration for the institutions interested in cleansing the financial industry from crooks. He disclosed that the FSA regulates more than twenty-eight thousand firms. In 2006, the FSA fined Capital Financial Administrators Limited (CFA), a third-party administrator of collective investment schemes, £200,000 for poor antifraud controls over client identities and accounts. Since then, the firm had taken necessary measures to rectify its controls. He also disclosed that the FSA fined Nationwide Building Society £1 million for "failing to have effective systems and controls to manage its information security risks." A laptop containing confidential information of its customers was stolen from the house of one of

295 "Fraud Management in the Financial Services Sector," http://www.fsa.gov.uk/pages/Library/Communication/Speeches/2007/0220_ey.shtml.

its employees. Afterward, Nationwide adopted necessary measures to tighten controls around customer accounts.

In view of the recurrent fraud and constantly changing techniques by fraudsters, Edna Young's speech carried vital information, as follows:

1. Consumers should not deal with unauthorized firms, whose credentials must be checked.
2. False claims cost the insurance industry more than £1.5 billion a year.
3. In a survey, as many as 37 percent of participants admitted that they would not rule out inventing an insurance claim, and 47 percent admitted that they may make an exaggerated insurance claim!

In 2008, Paul M. Clikeman published the book *Called to Account: Fourteen Financial Frauds That Shaped the American Public Accounting Progression*. The book describes how fraudsters fooled and misled their auditors, how packages of bricks were counted into business stocks, how Equity Funding personnel forged sixty-four thousand phony life insurance policies, and how Enron fictitiously boosted its profits. These frauds shaped the accounting standards and controls in America.

Typical techniques used in the financial industry aim to lure investors to commit their cash by setting their goals for the following:

1. Retirement pension schemes
2. Starting a new business or self-employment
3. Planning a foreign holiday
4. Buying a house
5. Buying a new car
6. Providing for children's private education or university
7. Home renovation or improvement
8. Providing for private medication
9. Providing for family emergency
10. Providing for wedding expenses of children
11. Leaving inheritance for dependents and grandchildren

12. Paying off debts, credit card balances, and mortgages
13. Providing for any redundancy or unemployment
14. Making provision for the inheritance tax liability

Once the conman gets a feeling that the inquirer has shown some interest in investment products, he may bombard the investor with phone calls. The best way to recognize the conman is through his attitude and approaches. He will generate false hopes of double- and triple-figure growth. However, no investment is risk-free. If anyone promises that his products are risk-free, then his claim should be viewed with skepticism. At the same time, if anyone fails to disclose the level of risk (low or high), then he is not to be trusted. If he avoids discussing past performance of the funds, then he has something to hide. If he does not disclose anything about the profile and past experience of those who are managing the funds, then he cannot be relied on. If the prospective investor is lethargic and not inquisitive, then the conman can easily succeed in duping such an investor.

Conmen are well trained, smart looking, and well dressed, and they pose as being educated and successful in their fields. The best way to distinguish fraudsters from genuine stockbrokers or investment advisors is to check independently their credentials, creditworthiness, membership in a professional body or association, and past financial statements of their businesses. The potential investor should request from the company three to five years of accounts and annual financial statements of stockbrokers to ensure that they are financially sound and are not facing any bankruptcy. They may well turn out to be undischarged bankrupt. If in doubt, the investor must ask as many questions as possible to clear his or her doubts, not caring a bit that such questions may sound stupid or embarrassing. If the investor gets vague replies, then he or she should extend those inquiries through third-party sources.

The same procedure should also apply when choosing investment products. Instead of placing blind trust in stockbrokers, conduct an independent investigation of the products through a third party like a bank or legal advisor. The investor should ensure that the proposed investment products are under the supervision of the FSA in the United Kingdom and the SEC in the United States. However, this alone does not guarantee that these products are free from abuse.

If any firm of stockbrokers indulges in any hot tips, either through phone calls, e-mails, or Internet blogs, then this should immediately raise suspicion of the would-be investor, who should never take anything for granted. He or she should not act on oral representations, which can be easily denied.

The investor should insist on studying three to five years' worth of past financial statements of the promoted investment product. If the investor does not understand the complexities contained therein, then he or she should seek professional advice. Any hasty decision taken might be regretted later on. The conman may put pressure on the investor to make a quick decision or miss a golden opportunity, in which case the investor should be able to boldly refuse and ask the stockbroker how much of his own personal money he is putting into the funds to avail himself of the opportunity that is not to be missed. The answer, in all probability, will be zero.

The most common fraudulent schemes are as follows:

1. Pyramid schemes, where the fraudster uses money supplied by subscribers to pay off earlier subscribers, with a guaranteed amount being paid to him at the addition of each subscriber. When the scheme gets exhausted, with no new subscribers entering the game, the scheme collapses, and many, if not most, subscribers end up losing money in this phony scheme.
2. Boiler rooms, where call centers are created most probably in foreign countries, promoting scam schemes and penny shares.
3. Pump-and-dump (P&D—(see glossary of terms) penny stocks, where promoters buy a huge quantity of penny shares and then sell them at highly inflated prices. They promote these schemes through other stockbrokers, the financial press, websites, and phone calls. When the price of the stocks is driven high enough, the promoters dump the stocks by selling their holdings. As a result, the prices collapse, and investors end up losing money.
4. Offshore funds, which are sold under very attractive ventures. Conmen may get their shady schemes registered in offshore centers to escape any legal accountability and controls.
5. Fraudulent promissory notes and currency investment promoted by fraudsters in the name of foreign countries or overseas-registered schemes.

6. Fake promise of a high rate of return, where the rate offered on the proposed scheme is more than the market rate, or where a large deposit is demanded to buy a stock that is nonexistent.
7. False promise of buying a stock, claiming to command advantage of insider information, before it opens for public offer and allotment.

Almost all of the aforementioned schemes may have a connection with organized crime, where eventually the promoters may disappear and live a luxurious life with the looted money.

CHAPTER 13

BURSTING OF THE DEBT BUBBLE

The international banking crisis of the 1980s was caused by banks' imprudent lending policies. The excess capital arising from the boom in oil prices of the 1970s found its way into banks in the West from the oil-producing countries of the Middle East. These excess deposits encouraged the banks to lend to oil-importing countries having no reliable credit worthiness.

International debt has played a major part in causing stock market crashes. The US federal government debt in 1987 totaled $2.35 trillion, and state and local governments had a combined debt of $550 billion. The former spent $165 billion, and the latter spent $55 billion servicing the debts.[296]

There is a great appetite for debt in developing countries too. In the early eighties, Mexico issued warnings that it could not repay its debt of $77 billion.[297] This did not affect wealthy Mexicans maintaining assets worth $84 billion abroad.[298] In the aftermath of the oil-price inflation of the seventies, banks showed eagerness to lend money to Mexico. Government and businesses borrowed heavily. When oil prices declined, the country was left with a heavy debt burden. Despite the fact that the borrowing country was an oil producer, it did not benefit from the global economy as much as the lending countries did.

The Philippines' late dictator, Imelda Marcos, allowed facilities for foreign corporations in free trade zones, with a right to repatriate a 100 percent profit in foreign currency. With cheap labor lavishly available, American corporations established assembly plants in Philippines. The World Bank acclaimed Marcos's economic policies.

296 Wood, 10.

297 Geisst, 326.

298 Engler, 128.

As a result, loans were approved "eight times greater than those it had given in the previous twenty years," as quoted by Engler.[299] After ten years, in 1982, the International Monetary Fund (IMF) acknowledged that the growth rate of the Philippines was the lowest in Asia. Engler comments that the IMF applied Ricardo's theory of comparative advantage and believed that international trade would benefit. However, Ricardo had qualified his theory; it would apply only when there was a restriction on the mobility of capital. In this case, there was none. When the crunch came, Marcos absconded with millions of dollars, leaving behind a debt of $26 billion.[300]

Developing countries had learned nothing from each other's experiences. Britain had encouraged Egypt to grow cotton in the pre-colonial era, a situation that was characterized by comparative advantage, and to pay its loans in the process. Cotton was produced for Britain's textile mills, but food production declined. Eventually, Egypt could not repay its debts, so Britain took charge of the country in 1882.[301]

The inequity of globalization manifested in affluent countries. The richest 20 percent of the world's population benefited from 83 percent of the global GDP in 1989. The poorest 60 percent benefited from less than 6 percent of the world's GDP.[302] Even in the case of countries like Singapore, South Korea, and Taiwan, which had readily succumbed to free market economies, there was strict control over capital movement out of the country. South Korea decreed a death sentence for the offense of smuggling foreign currency out of the country.[303] When a country is in heavy debt, some controls have to be enforced. But if corrupt government officials go on burdening the country with foreign loans and then help themselves by smuggling a large chunk into their offshore accounts, the country may not come out of murky waters.

Some third-world countries benefited from loans by increasing their agricultural output through mechanization and improved methods. Supply overtook demand. As a result, prices fell sharply. Revenues proved to be insufficient to service the debts. As a result, a vicious circle of debt crisis was set in motion. This gave a poor credit rating to the countries concerned, triggering a downfall in their stock markets.

---

299 Ibid.

300 Ibid., 130.

301 Ibid., 133.

302 Ibid., 137, quoting the *United Nations Human Development Report 1992.*

303 Ibid., 138.

Brazil entered into a spider web of debts when the military government took over. At that time, one-third of Brazilians suffered from malnutrition. But twenty years after the IMF-sponsored development programs, two-thirds suffered from malnutrition.[304] From 1979 to 1985, Brazil paid $70 billion in interest. In February 1987, Brazil stopped paying interest on debt.[305] Brazil owed foreign banks $113 billion.[306] The situation was reminiscent of Argentina's debt crisis, which was unmasked in mid-July 2001. Argentina, it was declared, might default on its debts of $120 billion. This news, as in 1987, sent shock waves through the world's stock markets.

Debt is an integral part of social and political problems. Despite the country's rocketing debts, fifty thousand Brazilians, out of a population of 165 million, owned everything in the country,[307] and four million peasants shared only 3 percent of the land.[308] By 1990, Argentina, Nicaragua, and Peru recorded inflation of 2,000 percent. Brazil had an annual price inflation exceeding 2,000 percent in 1994.[309]

The world bond market—the vehicle for government borrowing—grew from less than $1 trillion in 1970 to $23 trillion in 1997.[310] Between 1983 and 1989, a boom in borrowing in Japan gave way to speculation in commercial and residential properties. Mortgages extended to two or even three generations. In 1998, the credit bubble burst, and the property market fell. Japan tried to revive its markets by persistently lowering the borrowing rate. Yet even an interest rate of 0.5 percent flagrantly failed to revive the bond and equity markets.[311]

Warburton cites several cases in which the issue of bonds by corporations proved detrimental. Procter & Gamble, a US conglomerate, entered into a complex arrangement to save interest of $7.5 million over five years. Instead, it ended up with the cost of $157 million on its borrowings of $200 million.[312] The phenomenal bad-debt

304 Ibid., 135.
305 Wood, 113.
306 Ibid., 11.
307 Bales, 124.
308 Ibid., 129, 142.
309 Johnson, 228–31.
310 Warburton, 3–4.
311 Ibid., 11.
312 Ibid., 5.

burdens in the world banking system caused one thousand bank failures in the eighties. The number was "five times the number of failures in the previous four decades."[313]

Describing the chain of economic disasters the Asian Pacific countries were facing in 1997, Blustein writes that South Korean officials disclosed reserves amounting to $24 billion to the IMF. But usable reserves were only $9 billion and were declining at the rate of $1 billion a day because foreign banks were demanding repayment of loans. The figure that was disclosed to the IMF a few months earlier showed $70 billion owed to foreign banks. Then all of a sudden, the number jumped to $120 billion, payable in weeks. The default was imminent, and this would have damaged South Korea's creditworthiness. The IMF mission had earlier failed to probe or question the credibility of the figures in the first place. It had just accepted the South Korean officials' version at face value.

Blustein further discusses the debt crisis, which had deteriorated to an extent that Thailand received funds of $17 billion, Indonesia $33 billion in October 1997, Russia $22 billion in July 1998, and Brazil $41 billion in January 1999.[314] The IMF funds were used mainly to repay interest and principal to Western banks. Yet Blustein is full of praise for the IMF, the Federal Reserve, and the "policymaking wizards of Washington" for saving Southeast Asian countries from economic meltdown. Alas! The same brilliant wizards remained paralyzed in the face of the economic catastrophe that had befallen the United States since 2007. They remained passive when faced with the worst financial menace since the Great Depression of the 1930s.

Vividly describing the IMF's staffing arrangements, Blustein writes that the organization employs staff from 120 countries, a quarter of whom are from the United States. He refutes conspiracy theories attributed to the IMF by citing an example of the appointment of IMF's first deputy managing director, Stanley Fisher, who occupied the post from 1994 to 2001. He had excellent relations with the bosses at the US Treasury and was a successful member of the only Jewish family among the four hundred white people in a predominant black population of the former Rhodesia. He studied Hebrew on an Israeli kibbutz and was commissioned by the US secretary of state George Shultz to advise the Israeli government on economic matters. His success

313 Johnson, 261.

314 Blustein, 9.

in getting the Israeli economy back on track in 1985 earned him a post of chief economist at the World Bank in 1988.[315]

Because the controlling votes at the IMF and the World Bank were held by the United States, the US government appointed the top executives of these organizations. Under the undemocratic structure of G-7 (in those days), the US dictates always prevailed.[316]

Blustein describes the scenario of Mark Mobius, who traveled 250 days a year to "proselytize" vigorously for his emerging markets investment, which had grown one-hundredfold from 1987 to 1997. By 1995, one thousand mutual funds had emerged to invest in emerging markets, in which private capital jumped from $42 billion in 1990 to $329 billion in 1996.[317]

All the past experience of boom-and-bust was forgotten as private investors, banks, and insurance and pension funds fell for promises that were too good to be true. In the 1820s, there was a rush for South American gold mining shares in Britain. By 1826, when these shares crashed, Benjamin Disraeli, the British prime minister, suffered a nervous breakdown. Then there were crashes in the 1850s, 1870s, and 1890s.[318]

Yet very few, if any, of the new investors bothered to study the plight of their predecessors until they themselves headed for a steep fall off the cliff. In their enthusiasm to multiply their accumulated excess capital, quickly turned millionaires tend to forget that it is the job of the opportunist fund managers, financiers, and brokers to fill gullible investors with false promises, as if a history of investments starts anew with the entry of new investors. There is a whole range of black pages or dark ages that affect the financial world, and new investors should have bothered to become fully conversant in them instead of ending up in a bust situation.

The origin of the banking and financial crisis that hit Thailand's system was Thailand's commercial banks' lending to property developers, which jumped from $89 billion in 1992 to $204 billion in 1996. Finance companies were stuck with $4.8 billion in loans on margin lending to stock market speculators.[319] History was repeating

315 Ibid., 30–32.

316 Ibid., 35–36.

317 Ibid., 39–41.

318 Ibid., 43.

319 Ibid, 56–57.

itself, with the same old story unfolding that the borrowers could not repay the loans. Before dumping their capital in the fragile system, international investors should have considered the corruption factor in Thailand and other emerging markets, including Russia. In 1996, the Bangkok Bank of Commerce was in deep trouble. But much more troubling was the fact that the central bank had been aware since 1993 of the existence of defunct loans the bank was carrying on its books.[320] But it remained quiet because the unrecoverable loans were given to the bank's insiders, including its bosses and influential politicians and lawmakers, against whom no law could be enforced.

From the detailed discussion of Blustein on the financial menace in Thailand in 1990s, one could perceive that the focal point of the crisis revolved around legalized money laundering or the free flow of capital, a hike in the interest rate, and over lending, based on the interest-rate differentials in different currencies. He writes that George Soros earned $1 billion in 1992 by successfully betting that the pound's decline outside the limits set on European currencies was inevitable.

From the description of hedge funds, it is clear that they are not beneficial to the economy as such. Rather, they are "open exclusively to the rich, which means they escape regulations" and "seek to hedge their bets."[321] This speaks volumes about the fact that hedging is a process by which bets on short selling are protected with additional bets. As Thailand's currency was victimized by short sellers in 1997, Thai authorities came under increased pressure from the IMF to devalue. Soros's Quantum Fund, J. P. Morgan, and Goldman Sachs were all involved in betting on its fall. Thai authorities put a ban on lending the Thai currency outside the country. As a result, the hedge funds that had sold short were stuck with colossal losses. The interest rate jumped to as much as 1,500 percent.[322] Thailand adopted very tight measures to protect its currency. The Bank of Thailand was lending secretly to financial institutions in the country that were underperforming or not performing at all.

Effectively, the Thai government was bailing out the rich and powerful in the establishment who had taken unwarranted risks and was leaving small and medium-sized businesses to suffer the consequences of officials' negligence and corruption.

320 Ibid., 58.

321 Ibid., 61–62.

322 Ibid., 71.

The IMF staffer had failed to foresee the severity of the disaster as in the cases of Indonesia and South Korea. Between 1997 and 1998, the Indonesian currency under President Suharto's despotic reign had declined by 85 percent.[323] The economic boom and high standards of living the country had once witnessed started declining as the dictator was bent on misusing the country's resources to promote nepotism and favoritism. As the average Indonesian suffered, members of Suharto's family minted millions. Four percent of Indonesia's Chinese population owned 40 to 70 percent of the country's wealth.[324]

Indonesia's economy started on a disaster course when, under the direct influence of the despot, the banks started giving further loans to borrowers that were already defaulting on paying interest and principal on previous loans. The financial statements made provision of bribe payments to the bank officers.[325] The story of Thailand was repeated in Indonesia. As the Indonesian currency declined, Indonesian borrowers who had heavy foreign debts needed to buy foreign currencies at very high rates to repay their loans. Only when the economic meltdown had dawned on the country did Suharto care to wake up from his long slumber by asking the Malaysian Prime Minister Mahathir Mohamad, "What is the role of all these speculators?"[326]

Under these circumstances, in which speculators had ripped off the economy of the country, some banks had to be closed down in a similar way as when President Franklin Roosevelt ordered the closure of seven thousand US banks permanently, and then went along in reassuring the American public that the rest of the banks were safe and sound.[327]

At about the same time as the economic crisis was boiling up in Thailand and Indonesia, a crisis on a mammoth scale was unfolding in South Korea for similar reasons. Blustein wrote, "From 1994 to 1996, Korea's liabilities to foreigners soared by more than £45 billion".

When a country's economy is in trouble and the interest and principal on loans fall due to foreign lenders, mostly American financial institutions, a rescue mission

---

323 Ibid., 82–87.

324 Ibid., 90–91.

325 Ibid., 94–95.

326 Ibid., 100.

327 Ibid., 108.

of the IMF is commissioned to find solutions. Suddenly, a big hole appears between the officially declared figures of reserves of foreign currency and the actual balance at the central banks. The excuse given, more often than not, is oversight or a difference between what is accessible and what is not. Even if the IMF mission discovers over declaration of foreign reserves that might not cover foreign debts, as it discovered in the case of Korea,[328] whatever measures the mission may take are unlikely to cause corrupt officials and bribe takers to mend their ways. On the contrary, they may take consolation in the fact that the mission has approval from its headquarters in Washington to issue further loans, albeit with conditions, such as devaluation of the currency, raising of the interest rate, and substantially permitting foreigners to compete unhindered in the money market by opening foreign-owned subsidiary banks or brokerage houses and public companies. Sometimes, when developing countries are on the verge of economic collapse, they turn to the IMF seeking desperate help, like Bolivia, where the inflation rate in 1985 was running between 24,000 and 60,000 percent.[329]

But Malaysia's Mahathir Mohamad had diagnosed the disease of the economic ills and hit the nail right on the head of global capitalism by blaming hedge funds and currency speculators for the economic crisis. He advocated the need to regulate the global capital market. But the IMF, controlled by the policy makers in Washington, chose to resort to pumping in rescue funds, such as $50 billion to Mexico for the prime purpose of repaying foreign debts.[330]

On the subject of the bursting of the debt bubble in 2007, George Soros lays the blame squarely at the doorstep of the Bush administration. He writes that $45 trillion worth of contracts were outstanding[331] amid the current credit crunch. Uncertainty loomed all over the financial industry, and the parties to the contract could not tell whether contractual obligations would be honored at all. This is because regulators allowed the creation of debts at unsustainable levels. He further writes that some weak elements in society, like senior citizens and "communities of color," as he calls nonwhites, were targeted and victimized into house-buying schemes they did not understand. In Maryland, for instance, 54 percent of African Americans entered into

328 Ibid., 130.

329 Ibid., 148–53.

330 Ibid., 164, 174.

331 Soros, 147.

subprime loans, compared to 47 percent of Hispanics and only 18 percent of whites.[332] It follows that in areas where the ethnic communities were poised to lose their home ownership, crimes were bound to multiply, making the entire neighborhood unsafe for the elderly and children.

Soros expresses regrets that Treasury Secretary Henry Paulson did not rescue Lehman Brothers but had to rescue American International Group (AIG). Within four days of Lehman Brothers declaring bankruptcy, the confidence of depositors dwindled, and there was an intensive run on money and the stock market. As a result, the Federal Reserve had to pump in $700 billion and extend a guarantee to all money market funds.[333]

Precisely as in the 1987 crash, the collapse of the financial markets post-September 2008 wiped out asset values from pension, charitable, and university funds. Soros writes that the boom progressed gradually, but the bust set in suddenly and sharply. He believes that trading in indices was as damaging to the economy and the financial markets as portfolio insurance, which caused the great crash of 1987.[334]

Foster and Magdoff explain the harsh reality of the capitalist system: there is a wide disparity between real income and spending of various income groups. Among the bottom 60 percent of the working class in the United States, workers spent all their income on consumption, whereas the high-income band spent a very small percentage on personal consumption.

The phenomenon of declining real wages in tandem with increasing consumption is explained as follows. Workers resort to increased borrowing to make ends meet. It follows that groups in the lowest income band are bound to default on repayment of their debt. As a result, personal bankruptcies in the first George W. Bush administration reached five million in the United States.[335] The ease with which low-income groups could borrow was leading the way toward the bursting of the debt bubble. House buyers were required to put down a mere 2 percent for mortgage lending, and sometimes no deposit at all. They were allowed to raise further loans on remortgaging their real estate. The US mortgage companies took a calculated risk by lending

332 Ibid., 149.

333 Ibid., 161.

334 Ibid., 233–36.

335 Foster and Magdoff, 27–32.

money on inflated values of the properties. This was not a real gain but unrealized paper profit. If profit was not realized, and in many cases it was not, then the borrower defaulted on repayment of the second or third mortgage. In this way, the mortgage companies were digging their own graves.

When the Federal Reserve reduced interest to stop the economy from falling into a deep recession, household debt multiplied by 75 percent from 2001 to 2005.[336]

Credit card debt soared, with no increase in real income. Unpaid credit card balances at the end of 2005 amounted to $8.38 billion in the United States.[337] Borrowing for buying automobiles and for paying tuition fees also soared. The frenzy over takeover bids and mergers broke all-time records, accompanied by an increase in debts.

From October to December 2005, new home-mortgage loans rose by $1.1 trillion, bringing the total of outstanding mortgage loans to $8.66 trillion.[338] Borrowing for consumerism or consumption goods does not increase wealth as do loans for investing in manufacturing machines, aircraft, ships, automobiles, or even military equipment. These investments create employment as well.

Manufacturing and selling military equipment and weapons provides opportunities for destroying and then rebuilding war-torn countries. There are arms- and weapons-producing countries that thrive in theaters of war. There are arms- and weapons-consuming countries that thrive on chaos and on civil wars. As a result, demand and supply sometimes reach equilibrium.

Japan and Germany were built on remnants of war destruction and grew to become industrially advanced nations. The nations that helped them rebuild benefited most, with their GDP shooting up, which turned them into world powers.

The United States, the largest debtor nation in the world, has run dual deficits—a current-account deficit and a balance-of-trade deficit—ever since 1980, reaching $700 billion, or $2 billion a day.[339] It could aggravate the problem beyond control if foreign countries decided to shift their US-based assets to other currencies. Because of the rising debts injected into the economy through surplus in petro dollars and low interest rates, the economic fundamentals in the US and European countries were shifting

---

336 Ibid., 50.

337 Ibid., 34.

338 Ibid., 35.

339 Ibid., 51–52.

away from productive sectors. In the 1960s, financial profits represented 15 percent of domestic profits in the United States. By 2005, they represented almost 40 percent.[340] Due to the availability of cheap loans and a range of financial products, many manufacturing companies started offering banking, insurance, and credit card services, from which they earned more profit than from their traditional productive sectors. General Motors Corp. lost money on car manufacturing, but its profits boomed in the mortgage business. Cheap debt created the potential to offer innovative new products in the form of collateralized loans or hedging or leverage, which in turn shot up the potential for speculation in derivatives and in world currencies around the clock, with an enhanced risk factor. Bets were placed on almost everything, including potential terrorist activity or assassination of a public figure.[341] This was amoral compared to straightforward trading on the stock exchange. Stocks traded on the New York Stock Exchange increased steadily from 19 million in 1975 to 109 million in 1985 and to a staggering 1.6 billion by 2006 on a daily basis, in addition to $18 billion bet in world currencies on a daily basis in 1977 to $1.8 trillion per day by 2009.[342]

If a mere rumor results in the meltdown of the stock market, one can envision what the ailing capitalism means in terms of billions in currency values being wiped out dramatically in a few seconds.

The figures of foreign exchange and currency derivatives are too terrifying to express in terms of potential disaster in the offing.

The notional amount of OTC derivatives at the end of June 2006 was $283 trillion—according to Foster and Magdoff, "more than six times all the goods and services produced in the world during a year's time."[343]

340 Ibid., 54.

341 Ibid., 57.

342 Ibid., 56.

343 Ibid., 58.

CHAPTER 14

RECESSION AND THE STOCK MARKET SLUMP

The first sector to be hit hard in a recession is the manufacturing sector. Steep falls in demand compel orders for goods to be canceled, and as a result, workers are laid off and manufacturing units are shut down. The service sector and especially the financial industry are the next to be hit. The expansion during a bull market backfires with full vigor. Takeovers and mergers tend to combine businesses that are quite different in nature under the control of the same management. A restaurant chain negotiates to take over a transport company. A transport company expands to own an insurance company. Companies supplying gas and electricity invade the telecommunications industry.

The "Millennium bug" phobia caused many companies to overinvest in computer technology, replacing their old systems. Consequently, in 1999, share prices of high-tech companies soared. This tempted institutional and small investors to buy high-tech shares when the market had peaked. As soon as the spiral of decline set in, shares started to fall in the double digits. In 1999, experts on Fleet Street, London's financial district, were warning of an imminent crash in the year 2000.

By 2001, US corporations by the dozens were closing down every week. But dealers and investment advisors were desperately trying to divert the attention of investors from the real issues. When asked about it in the media, they would say, "The overheated economy is slowing down" or "There is a correction going on in the market." Young graduates from American and European universities formed their dot-com empires, which made millionaires out of raw graduates. But the honeymoon was short lived. By the start of the fourth quarter of 2000, the cycle of bust was in motion. Market sustainability of dotcom companies collapsed. Many budding companies had to be liquidated.

One of the main causes for market depression at the beginning of the twenty-first century was the bursting of the high-tech and dotcom bubbles, whose negative repercussions were to be felt for a long time to come. The governments auctioned third-generation licenses (see glossary of terms) for billions of pounds.[344] Telecom giants competed to win the licenses. As a result, they ended up with huge debt that could not be supported by market demand. Investors became scapegoats for the disastrous decisions of governments and telecom executives. Yet disgruntled investors who lost heavily had to bear the burden of the bonus schemes of millions of pounds voted by the majority shareholders for the chief executive officers (CEOs) for their success in gaining the licenses.

Between 2000 and 2002, Wall Street lost $7 trillion, or 40 percent of value, in quoted shares.[345] The US economy went into a deep recession. Alan Greenspan, the Federal Reserve chairman, confessed that it was the worst bear market in fifty years. He blamed "irrational exuberance" and "infectious greed" for the hikes of the eighties and mid-nineties in the stock markets, which were now facing a backlash. The phrases he used fascinated many people and attracted comments from the public in more than four thousand pages posted on the web. An investor on Wall Street gave his lifetime savings of $700,000 to a professional stockbroker to invest. By April 2002, he was left with $403.95.[346]

Accountancy Age added a different dimension to the causes of the slump. It wrote that the defect was in the improper accounting for incentive stock options, which represented 80 percent of the payment schemes for US executives.[347] Writing in the ACCA's *Corporate Sector Review*, Michelle Perry quoted Sir David Tweedie, who said, "Seventy-five percent of the world's share options go to the top five percent of executives."[348] Therefore, he asserted, they needed only one deal at a bolstered profit to enjoy riches.

---

344 "Licensing of Third Generation (3G) Mobile Briefing Paper," https://www.itu.int/osg/spu/ni/3G/workshop/Briefing_paper.PDF.

345 Jack Kemp, "'Infectious Greed' and Other Miasmatic Diseases," *Empower America*, July 2002, http://www.empoweramerica.org/stories, accessed on September 15, 2002.

346 David Usborne, "Wall St. Brokers Reduced Life Savings of £490,000 to £282," *Independent*, July 23, 2001.

347 Duncan Hughes, "Now the Fed Enters Standards Battle," *AccountancyAge.com*, July 25, 2002, http://www.accountancyage.com/Analysis/.

348 Michelle Perry, "Share Options," *Corporate Sector Review*, ACCA, issue 42, October 2002.

Sometimes the complex share-option schemes that are designed are difficult for minority or outside shareholders to comprehend. It may transpire on close examination that the majority shareholders, who are mostly the directors, have designed the scheme in such a way that they benefit both ways while taking up the options, whether shares are rising or falling.

Unit trusts (see glossary of terms) are not quoted on the stock exchange, whereas investment trusts are. Apart from price fluctuations, investors might have to bear management charges and a spread between buy and sell. When the slump starts, the financial industry as a whole is affected, including unit trusts and investment trusts. There are so many variables in the stock market that its activities cannot be confined to formulas, statistical analysis, charts, or predictions. Human factors, which are not predictable, are the main player.

When the spiral of a bear market sets in, investors tend to switch their money from the stock market to the property market. As a result, prices of properties shoot up. Low interest rates attract new home buyers. An increase in demand pushes the prices higher. In the process, a property bubble develops until the interest rate starts going up or the stock market picks up the momentum. Exceptional uncertainties also help boost the demand for properties.

Apart from domestic factors, two scenarios that have emerged in the past three decades have made an impact on foreign investment in the United Kingdom in real estate, deposits, and investment in shares. First, after the 1973 Arab-Israeli war, the Arabs were convinced that, according to Strange, "their oil revenues were far safer in the Euro-market deposits than in the US government securities, or even in US corporation shares."[349] Second, Arab institutions invested £827 million in the European property market in 2001, as disclosed by DTZ Research. Comparatively, Arab investments increased by £875 million in commercial properties in the first nine months of 2002 in the United Kingdom alone.[350] What had changed so suddenly, and from where was the Arab money being pumped into the UK market? In the aftermath of the September 11, 2001, terrorist attacks on the World Trade Center in New York, the United States announced that fifteen of the nineteen suicide hijackers were Saudi nationals. This was followed by the filing of $1 trillion in lawsuits against Saudi royal

349 Strange, 44.

350 Quoting from *Daily Reckoning*, Paris, November 27, 2002.

family members and other wealthy Saudis for allegedly aiding terrorism. Accusations in the US press and counteraccusations in the Saudi press entered the phase of a war of words. This could have been one of the destabilizing reasons for transferring Arab assets from the United States to the United Kingdom.

Corporate Governance

The corporate world is not only becoming increasingly complex and impersonal, but the power it musters may, at times, hold governments at ransom. Berle and Means describe vividly the power of the multinational corporate world: "The rise of the modern corporation has brought a concentration of economic power that can compete on equal terms with the modern state—economic power versus political power."[351] In the 1960s, when US business was booming, corporate executives fetched salaries that were forty times more than those of an average factory worker. When US business declined in 1990, the salaries of executives shot up and were eighty-five times more.[352] The CEO of Time-Warner was paid $78 million in 1990. Herschel Hardin, author of *The New Bureaucracy*, wrote, "This was more than twice the combined wages and salaries of 605 publishing division employees laid-off the following year as a cost-cutting measure."[353]

Even during a biting recession, when corporations suffer colossal losses, CEOs walk away with millions of pounds in golden handshakes on resignation or retirement. In recent times, some CEOs have seen the shareholder equity in their companies wiped out by more than 90 percent. This could mean that there was no business strategy or crisis plan in place. The CEOs neither were prudent nor took precautionary measures to protect shareholders' interest. Therefore, the fact that directors have a fiduciary relationship to shareholders remains empty words. The apologetic attitude tends to indicate that if shareholders are not happy, they can always vote out the directors in the general meetings. But in the general meetings, the directors themselves, who more often than not are majority shareholders, can easily overrule minority shareholders and continue earning huge salaries and bonuses.

---

351 Strange, 36–37.

352 Engler, 157, quoting Herschel Hardin, *The New Bureaucracy* (Toronto: McLelland & Stewart, 1991).

353 Ibid., 157, quoting *Globe and Mail*, September 26, 1991.

Figures released on August 20, 2001, as reported on TV networks, showed that salaries of fat cats in FTSE 100 companies increased by 15 percent, to £1.06 million basic, plus a 46.9 percent bonus. The figures were based on the research of a major accountancy firm in Great Britain. In view of underperformance of these companies, critics believed the directors' salaries and benefits should be performance related.

The *Financial Times* carried a detailed report listing top executives and directors who made millions from the bankruptcies of their companies. One such US Corporation was Exodus, which at the height of dotcom boom was valued at $30 billion. In two years, it became bankrupt. Yet its directors were the main beneficiaries because they had been given generous share options. The share price of Exodus jumped by 985 percent in a year. Revenues increased between 1999 and 2000 for a six-month period, from $73 million to $314 million. This became a ripe scenario for insider trading by the executives.[354]

The *Financial Times* investigation revealed that the executives of the twenty-five biggest doomed companies had milked $3.3 billion in salaries, share options, and bonuses, collected just in time for the companies to face insolvency. According to one *Financial Times* reporter, the "barons of bankruptcy show that failure also had its rewards."[355] FT.com demonstrated how sixty-one top management personnel ended up collecting $10 million each as their corporations became bankrupt from January 2001 to August 2002, in the midst of the stock market meltdown.

Some CEOs had their loans forgiven.[356] In the aftermath of the downfall of Enron, investor confidence was badly shaken. President George W. Bush intervened to restore trust and to champion "highest standards of conduct" in corporate governance. In the face of negative publicity affecting the company reputation, directors tend to serve their selfish interests first—as one author wrote in a journal, "assessing when to exercise options or sell shares."[357]

---

354 Caroline Daniel, "Insiders Who Managed to Get Out Just in Time," FT.com, July 31, 2002, http://news.ft.com/servlet/ContentServer.

355 Ien Cheng, "Survivors Who Laughed All the Way to the Bank," FT.com, July 30, 2002, http://financialtimes.printthis.clickability.com.

356 Ien Cheng, "Executives in Top US Collapse Made $3.3bn," FT.com, July 30, 2002, http://financialtimes.printthis.clickability.com.

357 Colin Coulson-Thomas, "Communicating Success," *Corporate Sector Review*, ACCA, issue 42, October 2002.

Although in many cases of failure, executive dishonesty was blamed, the US administration retracted from holding CEOs legally responsible for "negligence" and sufficed with pinpointing the responsibility for "business judgments."[358] If executives make wrong decisions, then they tend to sell unpopular shares before the reporting quarters—March 31, June 30, September 30, and December 31. This saves them from being in the awkward position of having to justify to trustees or pension committees of pension funds the reason behind their decision to buy those shares in the first place.[359]

On the other side of the spectrum, the silent majority of investors tend to voice the need to regulate widely abused stock-option schemes by executives. But legislators, many of whom are directors of giant corporations, resist lending a sympathetic ear. In an informative article, Porter Stansberry cites a case of the US giant IBM, which bought back $9 billion of its own stock and issued instead $20 billion of loan stock. The balance sheet leverage occurred during the time of Lou Gerstner as the company's CEO, from 1993 to 2000. The writer questions the motive for such a risky move, which was to cost IBM 8 to 12 percent interest, when it got away with paying only a 1 percent dividend to shareholders. One of the answers can be traced to the stock options of five hundred million stocks the CEO received as a result of a mere gearing (see glossary of terms) of the company's capital. After the CEO's departure, IBM confessed that it had boosted its operating revenue.[360]

A survey published by Hewitt Bacon and Woodrow discovered that eighty-two of the FTSE 100 companies operated share-option schemes, which allowed, according to one *Financial Times* writer, "up to 700 percent of base executive pay."[361]

---

358 Andrew Hill and Peter Spiegal, "Feeling the Heat," FT.com, May 9, 2002, http://news.ft.com/servlet/ContentServer.

359 Walters, 237.

360 Porter Stansberry, "The Debt Generation," *Daily Reckoning*, Paris, November 27, 2002.

361 Tony Tassell, "Executive Pay 'Still Not Made Clear to Investors,'" *Financial Times*, November 27, 2002.

CHAPTER 15

CASE STUDIES OF CORPORATE FAILURES

Enron

Enron is a classic case of flagrant abuse of the system, which has been invigorated in the twenty-first century although rules and regulations are far more stringent than in the seventeenth century. Enron's shares crashed from $82 to less than $1 per share in one year. The life savings and pensions of hundreds of thousands of people were wiped out. But the executives safely sold their own holdings and voted $100 million bonuses for senior personnel before the corporation, worth $80 billion, fell on its face.[362]

The Justice Department and Congress began investigation as the company filed for bankruptcy on December 2, 2001. Several factors were held responsible for the crash. It was alleged that Arthur Andersen, the auditing firm, was an accomplice in hiding the company's debts. This immediately brought into question the professional duty of care toward shareholders. The auditors were also accused of destroying key documents.[363]

President George W. Bush reacted by proposing that independent directors should be in majority on the board and that shareholders should approve share options. But the insiders who control majority shares can approve any options under the sun in their own favor. The after-event measures President Bush proposed included allowing the SEC to freeze "improper payments" to executives while the investigation continued.[364]

---

362 "Downfall of an $80bn Firm," *Observer*, January 13, 2002, http://www.guardian.co.uk/enron/story.

363 David Teather, "Duncan Denies Ordering Enron Shredding," *Guardian*, May 18, 2002, http://www.guardian.co.uk/enron/story.

364 "Bush Urges 'New Era of Integrity,'" *Guardian*, July 9, 2002, http://www.guardian.co.uk/bush/story.

What is proper and improper remains debatable. But President Bush made the point that "more scandals are hiding in corporate America." The SEC disclosed that the president himself had failed to file his 1990 sale of $850,000 worth of shares in Harken Energy. The share price plunged two months after the president sold his shares. Because he was the company director and also a member of the audit committee, his trading prompted investigation by regulators. The White House acknowledged that the rules were violated.[365] Once again, the auditors' professional duties came into the limelight. Press reports also exposed suspect dealings of Vice President Cheney.[366]

One of the controversial issues in politics that has repercussions in the financial world is the subject of donations to political parties. Enron admitted that it had spent $2.5 million to lobby the Bush administration in the first six months after the election and had supported Bush's election campaign.[367] This proves that there is a vested interest of the corporate world in politics.

With politicians on their payrolls, some arms-producing corporations can easily get away with producing weapons of mass destruction, like chemical weapons, and supplying them to proxy nations so that demand may remain buoyant as these weapons are used on helpless and poor people. The same politicians then give statements to the world media and the United Nations expressing their concern about violations of human rights!

Enron investigators questioned certain personalities at the center of the US administration. The insider dealings and contracts of the US Army secretary Thomas White came under scrutiny.[368] Apart from political connections, another field of inquiry concerned intercompany financial transactions between companies registered onshore and those registered offshore in unregulated financial centers. In this case, Enron was said to have "hidden huge debts in offshore ventures."[369] It would

365 "Bush on Back Foot over Corporate Past," *Guardian*, July 2002, http://www.guardian.co.uk/enron/story/.

366 Paul Krugman, "How Bush Firm Used Accounting Scam," *Guardian*, July 9, 2002, http://www.guardian.co.uk/enron/story/.

367 Mark Tran, "Enron Admits Spending $2.5m on Lobbying," *Guardian*, March 8, 2002, http://www.guardian.co.uk/enron/story/.

368 David Teather, "FBI Investigates Army Secretary's Enron Dealings," *Guardian*, April 16, 2002, http://www.guardian.co.uk/enron/story/.

369 David Teather, "White House Faces Subpoena," *Guardian*, May 23, 2002, http://www.guardian.co.uk/enron/stories.

seem that regulations remain lax in offshore centers to accommodate flagrant abuse and financial crimes.

The *Guardian* published special reports tracing the link between members of the Bush administration and key figures at Enron. A clash of interest featured prominently in the Enron crash. A top economic advisor in the Bush administration was a former paid consultant at Enron. The secretary of the army was a former Enron vice president whose shareholdings were valued at between $50 million and $100 million. The auditors made "errors of judgment," though they were paid $52 million in fees. The elaborate report carried a profile of seventeen political figures who were directly or indirectly involved in the scandal.[370]

The aftereffects of the scandal were felt in the world's stock markets. Enron was the world's largest energy trading company and America's seventh largest corporation. It controlled 25 percent of the world's gas and electricity business. But the financial trouble was already brewing when Enron wrote off $1.2 billion of shareholders' equity in October 2001. As the spider web unraveled, Congress declared that it would sue the White House for refusing to disclose details of meetings Enron executives had with Vice President Dick Cheney. Enron was implicated for bribing even Indian politicians in the country's biggest corruption scandal.[371]

The Senate committee unveiled that Citigroup and J. P. Morgan Chase, the creditors of the estranged company, created "complex phony" transactions valued at $8 billion. The committee's investigation produced one million pages of documents. The names of some of the biggest financial institutions were mentioned as collaborators.[372]

Enron's collapse rendered thousands of people out of work, including five thousand of the company's employees in Europe. Many thousands of shareholders ended up with valueless certificates. In the aftermath of the Enron and WorldCom scandals, the Federal Bureau of Investigation (FBI) consulted a 1987-convicted stock market fraudster and criminal to find possible solutions.

---

370 "Special Reports Enron: Web of Intrigue," *Guardian*, http://www.guardian.co.uk/flash/.
Madeleine Bunting, "Fall of the arrogant", *Special Reports Enron: Web of Intrigue, The Guardian*, Jan. 22, 2002.

371 "Enron," *Guardian*, January 31, 2002, http://www.guardian.co.uk/enron.story/.

372 Jill Treanor, "Banks 'Knew of Enron Scam,'" *Guardian*, July 24, 2002, http://www.guardian.co.uk/Archive/Article.

In this context, the story of Barry Minkow is interesting. At sixteen years old, he was the youngest CEO millionaire on Wall Street. The mayor of Los Angeles had commended and honored his success, which included building a public company, ZZZZ Best, worth $280 million and employing fourteen hundred employees within a span of four years. But the apartment buildings he was supposed to be renovating did not exist at all, as fraud investigators found out. At twenty, he was sentenced to seven and a half years in prison for stock fraud. Then, working as a pastor in a local church and having cofounded the Fraud Discovery Institute, he said he believed fraud was "a means to an end." The media turned him into a celebrity. Finding grounds in common with Enron, he alleged that banks were ready to lend money if accounts "were done by Arthur Andersen." He played tactics with banks in the language they understood best. He employed reputable lawyers and accountants to impress the financiers. As shares in his company soared, he started stealing to fulfill his ambitions. Even in faking trading activities, he found similarity between his approach and Enron's.[373]

Disclosure requirements of statutory accounts are meant to act as a deterrent to fraud. Professional bodies and auditing standard boards publish accounting and auditing standards, with the rules to be applied in connection with company accounts. When auditors are unable to issue a clean audit report, they are expected, under professional ethical code, to qualify their audit reports. Yet many company frauds and forgeries have proved that flaws in the accounts played a significant role in misleading shareholders.

When the Enron bubble burst, the auditors were hoping to survive criminal charges. They offered initially to pay $750 million, which was later reduced to $60 million in settlement.[374] The directors owe duty of care to shareholders. If this is breached, then there are bound to be several legal implications. A former Enron executive pleaded guilty to bending accounting rules, money laundering, and fraud.[375]

Three former NatWest bankers were indicted for conspiring with two Enron executives to induce NatWest to sell its stake of $1 million in Enron partnership

---

373 "I Was a Teenage Fraudster," *Guardian*, July 11, 2002, http://www.guardian.co.uk/worldcom.story.

374 Peter Spiegel, "Andersen Parent Agrees $60m Enron Payout," FT.com, August 27, 2002, http://news.ft.com/servlet/ContentServer.

375 Peter Spiegel, "Former Enron Executive Pleads Guilty to Fraud Charges," FT.com, August 22, 2002, http://news.ft.com/servlet/ContentServer.

concerns. Then they went ahead in buying the shares and made a profit of $20 million on an immediate sell.[376] The contacts of NatWest bankers were with the Enron executive, who formed "off-balance-sheet partnerships" to conceal Enron losses.[377]

The Enron experience compelled analysts, financiers, and government and watchdog organizations to ponder on the lessons to be learned. The practice of paying credit rating agencies from the coffers of a company was construed as undesirable. Stockbrokers' responsibility also came under criticism, as their analysts were rating Enron shares as "buy" until the eve of the collapse. Conflict of interest of the investment bankers vis-à-vis the company was reviewed. If the research analysts who worked for the banks dared to issue a negative report, they faced the risk of losing their jobs because the banks saw this as a lost opportunity to win a high-profile client. Politicians' role also came under fire. Emphasizing the need for consultation between businesses and government, it was claimed that "special interests can even 'buy' legislation."[378]

The powerful lobby culture in the United States dominates the financial world just as it dominates the political world. In the aftermath of the Enron crash, many voices echoed that some drastic actions were needed to restore public trust. Yet the response of legislators and regulators to the increasing tide of corporate corruption was slow and sluggish. The Sarbanes-Oxley Act, which sought to reform corporate law, had to be postponed due to pressure from business lobbyists. It was eventually pushed through in July 2002. The corporate reform legislation was expected to have a deterrent effect. After August 14, 2002, the CEOs and financial directors of America's largest corporations were required to swear that the quarterly accounts of their companies were true.

Conflict of interest in the accountancy profession also came under attack. Observers wondered whether the disclosure standards in the United States were adequate.[379] Interest groups demanded transparency of information. The complicity of

376 Peter Spiegel, "NatWest Bankers Indicted for Enron Role," FT.com, September 13, 2002, http://news.ft.com/Servlet/ContentServer.

377 Lina Saigol, "Lavish, Laddish and the Lure of Lucrative Fee," FT.com, June 29, 2002, http://news.ft.com/servlet/ContenServer.

378 "After Enron—Agenda for Reform 2002—Unofficial Watchdogs Need Sharper Eyesight," FT.com, February 14, 2002, http://specials.ft.com/afr2002/FT.

379 "Enron: Who's Investigating Whom?" FT.com, January 18, 2002, http://news.ft.com/ft/gx.cgi/ftc.

external auditors in precipitating fraudulent behavior of corporate management was severely criticized. Much was to be desired in this area, as the experience of WorldCom proved later on.

WorldCom, France Telecom, Mobilcom, and Deutsche Telekom

On July 22, 2002, WorldCom filed for bankruptcy. The failure of WorldCom was twice the size of Enron in magnitude and four times the size of Global Crossing. It filed for bankruptcy to protect itself from its creditors. The diagnosis of the trouble was false accounting, as a result of which profits were enhanced by $4 billion. Revenue expenses were capitalized. Because the company was the United States' second-biggest phone company and the largest Internet provider, it was badly affected on two fronts: telecom meltdown and dotcom liquidations.

WorldCom kept expanding by acquiring sixty companies in fifteen years. In its heyday, it was worth $180 billion and had eighty thousand employees. The personal wealth of Bernie Ebbers, its CEO, was $1.4 billion. When the company fell, it was valued at $280 million, with seventeen thousand redundancies. The auditors, Arthur Andersen (not again!), claimed that vital information was withheld from them.[380]

The world's stock markets greeted the news with panic selling. President Bush yet again expressed concern over accounting practices of American corporations. From a profit of $1.4 billion, WorldCom ended up in a loss situation within a year. Investor confidence fell, reflected in the value of the dollar, which fell to its lowest level in two years against the euro. Before its collapse, the company had granted a massive loan of $408 million to its CEO.[381]

The WorldCom debacle sent shock waves across social and political domains. WorldCom served twenty million customers and supplied services to sensitive US national security. Shares that were once quoted on Wall Street at $50 were now not expected to fetch anything for shareholders. The company's total debt went up to $40

---

380 Mark Tran, "WorldCom Goes Bankrupt," *Guardian*, July 22, 2002, ttp://www.guardian.co.uk/Archive/Article/.

381 David Teather, "$4bn US Fraud Scandal Sparks Market Turmoil," *Guardian*, June 27, 2002, http://www.guardian.co.uk/Archive/Article/, accessed on July 24, 2002.

billion, owed mostly to large financial institutions.[382] The FTSE 100 index greeted the news by wiping out £55 billion from the value of its companies. It was the second largest fall on the LSE since the crash of 1987.[383]

WorldCom's decision to file for chapter 11 bankruptcy was a blessing in disguise because it meant that it could draw $2 billion from a debtor-in-possession package. Yet its unsecured creditors had to put up a fight to be paid anything at all out of $2.65 billion owed.[384]

Investors' reactions adversely affected the credibility of CEOs of giant corporations. The disclosure that WorldCom had lent its CEO more than $400 million for margin trading spread salt on wounds. Ebbers's lawyers claimed that "the chief executive of a company with sixty thousand employees can't know about every decision." Paradoxically, though, the CEO had enough time to monitor on video employees clocking in late for work and from breaks! The special report enlisted cost-saving devices that he personally supervised, which were infinitesimal in comparison with his own abuses.[385] This was a practical demonstration of the idiom "penny wise and pound foolish."

A preliminary report prepared for the court hearing by Richard Thornborough disclosed that the attempted takeover of Sprint by WorldCom was "at least partly designed to trigger large merger-related charges." When regulators blocked the proposed merger, $3.8 billion in expenses was capitalized to enhance the profit.[386] Maneuvering the figures through creative accounting resulted in corporate failures. The expenses that should have been charged conventionally to profit-and-loss accounts or income statement were treated as capital expenses to inflate profit figures artificially.

---

382 Jill Treanor, "$40bn in Debt—and Counting," *Guardian*, July 23, 2002, http://www.guardian.co.uk/worldcom/story/.

383 Neil Hume, et al., "FTSE Closes Down below 4,000 as Bush Intervention Fails," *Guardian*, July 16, 2002, http://www.guardian.co.uk/bush/story/.

384 Peter Thal Larsen, "The Job of Salvage Set to Begin," FT.com, July 22, 2002, http://news.ft.com/servlet/ContentServer.

385 Stephen Kirchgaessner and Peter Thal Larsen, "Life under Watchful Eye of Ebbers," FT.com, August 25, 2002, http://news.ft.com/servlet/ContentServer, accessed on September 15, 2002.

386 Peter Thal Larsen, "Court Report Sheds Light on WorldCom's Ways," *Financial Times*, November 5, 2002.

In the same period, France Telecom added to a series of scandals that hit the stock markets. The company recorded an $11.9 billion loss in the first six months of 2002. Its debt amounted to $68.3 billion. As the company announced that it was withdrawing its 28.5 percent stake in the German Mobilcom and writing off $7.1 billion, the latter ran into crisis. But although the government owned 55 percent of France Telecom, the company's shares fell by 70 percent within a year.[387]

Like Mobilcom, Vodafone, British Telecom, and Deutsche Telecom, France Telecom had entered into billions of dollars of debt to win the third-generation licenses. The slump in the telecom industry resulted in a "record-breaking number of bankruptcies and more than five hundred thousand jobs lost in the United States alone."[388] For economic reasons, the French government sought to rescue France Telecom, and in the wake of elections, the German government sought to rescue Mobilcom. At its peak, Mobilcom was worth €7 billion. By September 2002, it was worth €35 million.[389]

The part privatization of Deutsche Telekom was one of the biggest disasters or debacles of the twentieth century. Formed in 1996, it was the largest telecommunications company in Germany and in the European Union. Under its Israeli-born CEO, Ron Sommer, the company's debts rocketed to €67 billion ($68 billion), and the share prices plummeted in July 2002, resulting in a vote of no confidence by the supervisory board, the government, and the shareholders against the CEO. Because 90 percent of the share values had been wiped out under Sommer, this brought him to a clash with Germany's social democratic government, which at that time owned 43 percent of the company.

The government was facing an election in which it stood to be defeated if it failed to appease the aggrieved three million shareholders. But Sommer had powerful friends in Washington. Henry M. Paulson, head of the US bank Goldman Sachs, protested to the German company that if it sacked Sommer, it would have "negative consequences" on its business, as if everything had been positive and productive so far! This warning may have been seen as a threat by a foreign bank that it would take

387 John Leicester, "France Telecom Posts $12B Loss," Associated Press, September 13, 2002, http://Story.news.yahoo.com/news.

388 Christopher Stern, "Telecom Slump Continues," *Washington Post*, September 14, 2002, http://www.washington/post.com/wp-dyn/.

389 "Germany Plans Mobilcom Rescue," BBC News, September 13, 2002, http://news.bbc.co.uk/2/hi/business/.

its business elsewhere if Deutsche Telekom exercised its legal right to make changes in its top management. But the lobbying was so strong that moral values were turned upside down. More than eighteen thousand employees who stood to lose their jobs placed an ad in a newspaper asking the government, but not the foreign bank, not to meddle in the affairs of the company! The opposition parties alleged that Chancellor Gerhard Schröder was succumbing to the demands of small shareholders, as if the job of the opposition were only to look after the interest of majority shareholders or fat cats. They called the sacking of the CEO a "disaster."[390]

That was in 2002, but it is interesting to note that in his book *The Crash of 2008*, George Soros condemns, in a totally different matter, the approach of Henry Paulson, who by now occupied a celebrated government position. Soros writes, "Unfortunately, Treasury Secretary Henry Paulson reacted in a haphazard and capricious manner. That is how the situation spun out of control. After the bankruptcy of Lehman Brothers, he forced through Congress a $700 billion rescue package without any clear idea how it should be used to adequately recapitalize the banks."[391]

Coming back to Deutsche Telekom, under the company's former CEO Kai-Uwe Ricke, more than 1.5 million customers deserted to rival companies. As a result, the company had to lay off more than thirty thousand workers between 2005 and 2006. In 2002, within a few months, the share price had fallen from one hundred euros to twelve euros a share.[392] In the 2008 accounts, the net debt of the company stood at €38.2 billion. The share price of £40.60, at which the shares of Deutsche Telekom were allocated in June 2000 to the public, should have raised the eyebrows of investors, compared to £0.50 a share of BT when its shares were offered to the public.

Obviously, the so-called part privatization of Deutsche Telekom was meant to enhance the company's capital at a terrible cost to investors. When shares are issued at such a high denomination to represent goodwill that does not exist, then the interest of the public or outside shareholders is at stake. The insiders, the government, and some institutional investors may walk away laughing as minority shareholders are used as scapegoats. The audited accounts of a company are posted on the company

---

390 "Deutsche Telecom Chief Steps Down," DW Mode for Minds (editorial), July 16, 2002 http://www.dw-world.de/dw/article/0,1431,593333,00.html, accessed July 16, 2002.

391 Soros, 179.

392 http://en.wikipedia.org/wiki/Deutsche_Telekom.

website, and small investors should take some time to go through the jugglery of the white elephant's negative performance.

The story of British Telecommunications plc is equally disastrous. Initially, high profit margins attracted many competitors in the high-tech and telecom markets. But third-generation phones did not pick up, and the market was not prepared for sophisticated new technology. Even a prestigious blue-chip company like BT proved to be volatile. BT shares "more than doubled...between August 1997 and July 1998"[393] to more than nine pounds a share. In 1999, it rose to more than eleven pounds a share. But the company's debt burden and slump wiped out its share value substantially, by more than 90 percent. It remained at this level for more than nine years, although the company was trading and paying dividends too!

The Power of Transnationals and Its Impact on the Stock Market

In the eighteenth century, Adam Smith preached his economic philosophy that overproduction and unemployment are not matters to worry about in free markets. He believed that every increase in production would result in a corresponding increase in consumption. As production increases, wages tend to increase, pushing up demand for consumer goods. Correspondingly, as profits increase, savings and investments tend to rise. Smith believed that equilibrium is achieved when labor, capital, and resources are fully employed.[394]

In the early Industrial Revolution, the industrialists completely subdued and suppressed labor. Adam Smith opposed monopolies and joint stock companies. He rightly believed that self-interest interfered with market forces, although he was not against granting exclusive royal charters to companies providing utilities.[395]

Another serious challenge to the theory of market forces came from John Maynard Keynes, who refuted in his book *The General Theory of Employment, Interest, and Money* (1935) that investments and savings tend to equalize.[396]

---

393 Walters, 170.

394 Engler, 4.

395 Ibid., 6.

396 Ibid., 29.

The giant corporations wield the real power of the stock market. Allan Engler writes, "The combined profits of the ten most profitable transnationals (IBM, Ford, Exxon, Shell, General Motors, General Electric, British Telecom, Dow, AT&T, and Du Pont) at $40 billion equaled Iraq's entire gross national product in the year before the Gulf War."[397]

Economic globalization in the late twentieth century was also having its impact. "The one hundred largest transnationals controlled one-quarter of all global output."[398] Engler continues making amazing disclosures: "Seven oil transnationals (Exxon, Mobil, Texaco, Chevron, Amoco, Shell, and British Petroleum) control oil wells throughout the world and own huge reserves of natural gas, coal, and oil."[399]

Despite the recession in 1991, oil companies reported record profits, and despite the recession of 2000–2002 and strikes over hikes in petrol prices in Britain, again oil companies reported substantial profit figures while consumer interest suffered most.

Stock Markets and Ethical Investment Criteria

Reports from the Ethical Investment Research Service show that there is an increasing tendency among investors to select unit or investment trusts that meet their ethical criteria. Many investors do not like to invest in tobacco companies, breweries, businesses experimenting on animals, and businesses employing child labor. Exploitation of children in hazardous but lucrative industries has attracted world media attention in the past three decades.

Kevin Bales makes astounding disclosures in his well-researched study on child slavery in the modern world. He writes that among others, major cities in developed nations, like Paris, London, New York, Zurich, and Los Angeles, employ and brutalize thousands of children as house slaves. He warns that investment portfolios, mutual funds, and pension funds hold shares in companies that use child slaves in the developing world. "Slaves keep your costs low and returns on your investment high."[400]

---

397 Ibid., 39, quoting *Business Week*, July 17, 1989.

398 Ibid., 39.

399 Ibid., 40, quoting Michael Tanzer and Stephen Zorn, "Energy Update: Oil in the Late Twentieth Century," *Monthly Review*, 1985, 29–30.

400 Bales, 3–4.

In recent years, there has been a relocation of successful multinational companies that have established representative offices and assembly plants in India. Cheap labor is available there in abundance. "In India...there are between sixty-five million and one hundred million children aged fourteen and younger who work more than eight hours a day...About fifteen millions of these children are not child laborers but child slaves."[401]

In Africa, 90 percent of cocoa plantations in the Ivory Coast use slave labor. Cocoa is used in ice-cream flavoring and in the manufacture of chocolates enjoyed by millions of people around the world. But as one slave laborer who was never paid by the plantation owner for his work said, "It's like eating our flesh," as disclosed in A *Reporters* documentary on BBC,[402] which focused on the acute problem of child slavery in the Ivory Coast. Distressed and terrified parents believed that gangs employed by plantation owners had abducted their children. They said a TV program publicized the police record with names of kids who had disappeared. Children who managed to escape the plantations have provided conclusive evidence that the abuse does exist. Yet chocolate-consuming countries turn a cold shoulder toward the enormous human cost involved for the luxury they enjoy. Several manufacturers have adopted an apathetic attitude that the means justify the end of earning an attractive return on investment.

In the boom of the eighties, a strong Japanese yen and a robust economy prompted Japan to invest in Thailand. Japan and West Germany had provided exemplary models for rebuilding the economy from the post–World War II ashes. During the eighties, when the Far Eastern economy was flourishing, investment brokers were urging their clients to invest in the mutual funds of the tiger economies of South Korea, Hong Kong, Taiwan, and Singapore.

Amid widespread poverty and very low per capita income, the tourist industry in Thailand was attracting millions of tourists from developed and oil-rich countries at the cost of enslaved, brutally tormented, and coerced underage girls. Neighboring countries were involved in promoting the lucrative industry of child prostitution. As a result, AIDS became endemic in the region, and HIV infection spread to other

401 Ibid., 237.

402 Quoting BBC 24, May 27, 2001.

countries. The plight of underage children who are exploited by the multimillion-dollar tourism industry has been covered in several TV documentaries.

In the past fifty years, several African and Asian nations have been afflicted with civil wars. Autocrats and tyrants, supported by various powerful nations, have been engaged in wholesale looting of resources. "The ruling kleptocrats have paid enormous sums for weaponry, money raised by mortgaging their countries."[403] The shocking mass massacre in Rwanda took place with conventional weapons. But because there was enormous demand to supply the war-torn countries with arms and ammunitions, the corporations involved in their manufacture thrived in the stock markets.

Ethical criteria can be viewed from different angles. Eugene M. Propper explains several complications that investigators encounter while looking into financial fraud. The intimate personal and business connection among senior government officials, affluent families, and big-business executives can practically jeopardize the legal process. Information may be shuffled behind the backs of the investigators. To make things worse, interested parties may be represented by the same team of lawyers. At times, the parties under investigation muster considerable influence over the press.[404]

403 Bales, 12–13.

404 Eugene M. Propper, "International Corporate Fraud Investigations," Holland & Knight, March 16, 2000, http://www.hklaw.com/OtherPublication, accessed on October 26, 2002.

CHAPTER 16

SMALL INVESTORS—PAWNS IN THE GAME

Small investors can be easily enticed by crooks in the financial world through glossy brochures, aggressive mail shots, and telephone marketing, which are directed today, more often than not, from overseas call centers. Far from compliance with UK regulations, different types of pretenses and false claims are made to push shares in dubious funds or companies from overseas centers, outside the controls of watchdog organizations.

Small investors might be unaware that many stockbrokers do not have offices of their own. They operate from rented addresses, where they hire a room to see clients when the situation demands. They share with other small businesses administrative services, including a professional-sounding telephone answering service, with an assistant taking messages from clients very courteously. When a client phones, the standard reply heard over the phone is that the broker is in a meeting or out of office. But whether they rent an office space is beside the point. The stockbrokers buy ready-made, limited company services off the shelf, with a hired company registration office, which they are legally bound to have. With overheads kept at a minimum, they keep their addresses as mobile as themselves. Their burden is lighter as they sell intangible assets—stocks and shares. Their bread and butter is the brokerage or commissions they earn. Their earnings are dependent on deals for buying or selling shares on behalf of investors. If stockbrokers who are based in regulated financial centers get involved in pushing shares of companies registered in unregulated financial centers, then this conduct should raise investors' eyebrows. This may mean that the stockbrokers do not have the best interest of their clients at heart and that they are concerned only with earning hefty commissions from those dubious companies.

Subjective as it may sound, the main incentive for registering investment funds in unregulated offshore centers is not to avoid a heavy tax burden, as is often claimed, but to escape legal controls and regulations altogether. Therefore, investors might not be aware that if investment companies are dying to get a foothold in the so-called tax havens, they might turn their investment strategy or lack of controls into a nightmare for investors. The best way of investigating stockbrokers or investment companies promoting investment funds in unregulated centers is to study the statutory accounts of the stockbrokers or their firms for at least five years. These can be obtained from the Companies House[405] on payment of a small fee, which is worth it. At the same time, small investors have to be vigilant not to invest any money, no matter how glossy and well presented the promotion literature is, without studying the audited accounts of the fund managers, who might have employed deceptive and cunning tactics such as putting a public figure in place as the nonexecutive chairman of the fund or engaging the services of reputable bankers as custodians of the funds and appointing a household-name auditing firm as the auditors. These are all gimmicks that are divorced from reality. The whole purpose is to impress naïve investors.

Under the thought-provoking topic "Who Watches the Watchdogs?" Heller writes that in the 1960s, as fraud was committed under the watchful eyes of the watchdogs, they flagrantly failed to protect innocent investors from rogue elements in the market. He continues: "The overtrading and irresponsibility of the bankrupt brokers was of a piece with the misconduct of their fathers back in 1929."[406] He compares the plight of the investor in this situation to a patient who gets the attention of a gravedigger instead of a physician.[407] Under the subheading "I Know Something You Don't Know," he discusses the widely prevailing abuse in the stock market of using privileged insider information for personal gain.[408]

Back in the sixties, the international swindler Bernie Cornfeld promoted his Funds of Funds through salesmen who called themselves "financial counselors." They were able to collect from small investors $100 million within two years by touring vulnerable

405 Companies' House is the name of the government institution that houses all registered companies' records in the United Kingdom.

406 Heller, 194.

407 Ibid., 196.

408 Ibid., 201.

countries. The beneficiary of the brokerage fee was Investors Overseas Services, owned by Cornfeld.[409] He and his fellow directors misappropriated investors' funds lavishly for personal extravagance. When the scandal was unearthed, the investors lost heavily.

Small investors bear the brunt when markets fall and the economy goes into recession. Regulators in Britain discovered that more than half a million people were missold personal pension plans in the 1980s and early 1990s. The legal battle for these missold policies continues to this day. Small investors are constantly advised to adopt a long-term view to investment. It is said that in the long run, investment in shares and stocks outperforms all other investments. However, in the bear market, short-term expediencies are given priority over a "risk tolerant, long-term" investment strategy.[410]

On the investment side, a cautious investor would err on the safe side. But in the stock market game, how safe is safe? There is no safe answer. Small investors are bound to remain at a disadvantage compared to institutional investors, who have minute-by-minute access to share-price movements.[411]

Ian Rushbrook, manager of Personal Assets Trust in Edinburgh and one of the most successful professional investors, observes that the stock market is essentially "a nice casino." In this context, with the exception of a small minority of professionals, he says, it is "a loser's game."[412] In particular, small investors are at a disadvantage. They do not command resources that are available to professionals, including timely information,[413] which is the key to decision making and assessing risk and reward.

Small investors tend to rely on brokers' forecasts. Slater Walker, a British industrial conglomerate turned bank, had to close down after twenty-seven successful years. It admitted that "earnings and brokers' forecast can be easily manipulated."[414] Slater saw stock market players as "punters" who "bet seriously."[415]

At the start of 2002, stock dealers were predicting that stock markets had reached rock bottom, but the markets practically ignored the lowest interest rate of 1.75 percent in the United States for forty years. This indicated that investor confidence was

409 Chapman, 83–84.

410 Barry Riley, "FT Fund Management: Preparing for the Upturn," *Financial Times*, October 17, 2002.

411 Samuels and Wilkes, 544–45.

412 Davis, 216–18.

413 Ibid., 220.

414 Ibid., 174.

415 Ibid., 176–77.

badly hurt. Once share prices start rising, the investors jump the bandwagon to make a quick kill.

At the height of a bull market, small investors are lured to invest in risky shares. In universities, students with limited means start forming investment clubs. At work, colleagues start pooling their savings for investment purposes. In social clubs, friends start cementing their relationships for the sake of get-rich schemes. Everybody starts talking about shares doubling and tripling in value. The impressed investor enters the arena at that point and starts buying when the market is at its peak. But when the so-called market correction takes its course, it sheds its spectacular gains. Between 2000 and 2002, some high-tech and dotcom shares lost 99 percent of their value.

Whether the market is in a boom or bust cycle, it has totally failed to eradicate fraudulent scandals that rock the market. Ironically, the SEC—the powerful regulatory body in the United States—attracts bright young lawyers who then leave and open their own private practices with SEC credentials. In the 1990s, there were seventeen thousand registered investment advisors in the United States. Because of a staff shortage at the SEC, each registered member hardly got a spot check once a decade.[416]

With the information technology revolution, small investors are vulnerable in many ways. Sometimes interested parties plant false stories in the press. An Australian Senate committee investigation into a series of mining collapses discovered, according to Chapman, that stockbroker firms were instrumental in spreading word that a particular share was on its way up in an effort to offload their own shareholdings.[417] The shares that remained unsold were then allocated to client accounts under discretionary managed funds. Apart from overloading client accounts with shares the brokers knew would decline, insult was added to injury when they also charged brokerage to the clients.[418]

Small investors become subject to cold-calling scams, even from offshore call centers. Stockbrokers introduce obscure funds and then disappear. The Australian Securities and Investment Commission reported an increase in such activities,[419]

416 Chapman, 169.

417 Ibid., 164.

418 Ibid., 165.

419 William Barnes, et al., "Boiler-Room Problem Is Spreading across Asia," *Financial Times*, July 29, 2001.

according to *Financial Times*. Stockbrokers are known to exaggerate the growth prospects of the funds under their management.

A serious drawback to the interest of small investors is the process of spinning, whereby the merchant banks allocate, in public floatation, a certain proportion of shares to a company's senior executives. This is done with a specific purpose of attracting future business.[420] Swapping of favors creates a conflict of interest. This scenario raises a dilemma for regulators on how best to tackle the problem, which may damage investor confidence further.

In Britain, many loopholes were patched by the Financial Services Act 1986, repealed by Financial Services and Markets Act 2000, which forms the core legislation regulating the financial industry. Currently the Financial Services Authority is the umbrella watchdog organization. Firms wishing to conduct investment business in the United Kingdom have to be authorized by the FSA. However, many unauthorized firms are still conducting financial and investment business in the United Kingdom, according to a list produced by the FSA,[421] whereby the consumer deals with them at his or her peril, unprotected by law.

Ajit Singh of the University of Cambridge argues in his study that stock markets are a hindrance to development in developing countries.[422] John Maynard Keynes warned in 1936 that "when the capital development of a country becomes a by-product of the activities of a casino, the job is likely to be ill done."[423]

Professor Khurshid Ahmad writes that in 1952, the stock market created thirteen billionaires in the United States. In 1996–97, there were 170. The *Economist* magazine addressed the dilemma in 1998: "With over $150 trillion worth of derivatives circulating in the world and where the GDP of...188 countries of the world is only around $30 trillion, where are we heading?"[424] The major speculators are only two dozen big banks that control about 80 percent of the derivatives game.[425] This exposes the entire

---

420 Lina Saigol, "Spinning a Web for the City Regulators to Unravel," FT.com, October 24, 2002.

421 "Unauthorised Overseas Firms Operating in the UK," Financial Services Authority website, http://www.fsa.gov.uk/pages/Doing/Regulated/Law/Alerts/overseas.shtml.

422 Chapman, 96–97.

423 Ibid., 142.

424 Khurshid Ahmad, "Islamic Finance and Banking: The Challenge and Prospects," in *Review of Islamic Economics* (2000), 70, quoting *Economist*, May 30, 1998.

425 Ibid., 73.

monetary and economic system of the world to incalculable risk. The destructive experience of the conventional system is the best justification for the development of alternatives to the vagaries and moody turbulence of the stock market in the conventional economy.

Heller thoughtfully summarizes what is a perceptible reality in the market economy: "The overstatement of profits, the cooking of books...the false (but legally impeccable) prospectuses, the mismanagement that diverted cash to known and unknown destinations: all these could fit as easily into a cunning, deliberate plot to defraud as into a picture of incompetence magnified by greed."[426]

When shares crash on the market and the share prices of even giant companies worth millions of pounds fall by as much as 95 percent to become penny shares, the companies concerned not only survive but snub outside or minority shareholders by paying their executives millions of pounds in bonuses. Very few, if any, small investors would have wondered about the general apathy on the part of top management. The fact is that the company has allocated only a small portion of its issued share capital for the punters to gamble on the market. The rest of its issued share capital with a share-premium account is safe and sound from the vagaries and moody tremors on the market. It is an open secret that the supreme deity being worshipped in the corporate world is self-interest only. When there is a conflict between enhancing their own earning power and passing the benefit to outside shareholders, the latter is always sacrificed ceremoniously.

No small investor can come out of the market unscathed from this game of chance. And that is precisely what it is—a game of chance in which minority shareholders end up losing substantial values of their shareholding. On the other hand, majority shareholders or directors, who can tap in to insider information, know when to increase their holdings, subject to the articles of association of the company, at cheap or bargain prices, as outside shareholders may be facing annihilation of their investments. Subsequently, when prices increase, directors offload the shares they bought at bargain prices. There are several techniques at the disposal of directors to lure outside investors, such as the director's report presented at the annual general meeting and filed with the statutory accounts at the Companies' House, promising

426 Heller, 255.

growth potential and a healthy forecast for its earnings in the forthcoming years. But a forecast is a forecast, based on an expectation only, and it may never be realized. Or the forecast may turn upside down due to a downturn in the economy. Or if it is realized, most of it may be used to pay bonuses and salary increases to insiders, leaving only one weapon in the hands of outside shareholders: attending the annual general meeting and raising their voices, which can be easily subdued by the majority shareholders' vote.

Therefore, to claim that shareholders can always vote directors out of office is easier said than done. The controlling votes are in the hands of the directors by virtue of their being the majority shareholders. The management of the company may be compelled to carry out certain measures to save costs. But these measures are adopted only after the share prices of the company tumble in the market. Frequently, they are used as face-saving devices or as window dressing. The management team will never voluntarily surrender the bonuses it earned in preceding years, despite the fact that its fatal policies caused the company a loss of revenues, a loss of reputation, and a loss of credibility.

If the directors believe it is unlikely that the badly battered share prices of their company will rise again, then to add insult to injury, they may decide to reorganize the share capital of the company. Under this scheme, minority shareholders who have survived the drastic falls in share prices may be flushed out of the system altogether by having imposed on them the need to exchange a large number of their old shares for fewer new shares of larger denomination. Many companies resort to this type of legalized cheating because outside shareholders are not in a position to enforce their will.

Therefore, insiders who have a controlling interest get away with their manipulative maneuvers by claiming that the resolution was, after all, passed by shareholders in the annual or extraordinary general meeting. It is the small investors who always take the beating. In this way, investors may face double jeopardy in that they have seen their investment values reduced to peanuts. At the same time, the directors may decide to slap them on the face by requiring them to surrender several thousand of their shareholdings under the deception of getting new shares of higher value. From the directors' viewpoint, if the share price of the company quoted on the stock market keeps on appearing as a penny per share after having fallen from, say, £10 a share, this indicates that the directors have completely messed up the company's state of affairs. This is very damaging to their reputations and their future careers. So they may resort to reconstruction. Even if the shareholders succeed in kicking the directors out of office, the directors have earned enough bonuses to enjoy sunshine for the rest of their lives in the offshore islands of the West Indies.

In conclusion, it may be said that to counter this type of exploitation and daytime robbery, the matter has to be addressed from a moral perspective, by questioning the fairness and reliability of the system itself. If the system is open to abuse and it is costly for regulators to successfully prosecute abusers, then alternatives have to be explored in the interest of members of the public, who have been misused as guinea pigs for the supreme interest of the rich and the powerful.

Exploring the Alternatives

Amid the financial menaces that recur in perpetuity under the capitalist system, there are a range of dilemmas facing a conscientious investor. Here are some strategies for dealing with them:

1. Avoid, as much as possible, participating, expressly or by implication, in the schemes under which the poor become poorer and the rich become richer. That is precisely one of the characteristics of the game of chance being played in the global financial and stock markets that misallocates wealth and resources from the hands of the vast majority of the public into the hands of the most affluent minority.
2. Avoid becoming part of schemes that breed on misinformation and manipulation of the vulnerable. Many cases were cited in this study in which uninformed investors were exploited, deceived, defrauded, and misled by the stock traders/brokers because of traders'/brokers' vested interest in the products they sell. They earn hefty commissions for promoting certain dubious products.
3. Avoid the insatiable greed of the influential minority, who might have prospered through investments in the stock markets, which may lead them to invest in manufacturing of arms and a deadly arsenal. Apart from being a very lucrative investment, it can flourish only in theaters of war, where the majority being killed might be innocent people.

4. Do not invest in an industry that employs child labor and exploits vulnerable children by underpaying them or not paying them a fair wage at all. For example, in the carpet industry of India and Pakistan, child labor flourishes to pay for the never-ending exploitative debts of their parents and grandparents. The moneylenders charge exorbitant interest rates and continue exploiting borrowers for the rest of their lives. The study of Kevin Bale has many cases of this nature. The issue of child labor has attracted the attention of many human rights agencies and has been exposed in several TV documentaries in the West. Children are abducted, imprisoned, and forced to work in hazardous industries, under subhuman conditions, so that affluent capitalists can enjoy the finished products at very competitive prices. As long as manufacturers are able to redouble their profit margins, and their customers are able to enjoy the luxurious products, it does not matter to them that poor and helpless children in developing countries have to pay the price with their sweat and blood.
5. Do not invest in any funds that use cruel experiments on animals and result in the manufacture of certain luxurious cosmetics. The fact that pressure groups among mainstream communities are campaigning for the protection of the rights of animals against being used as guinea pigs shows the gravity of this problem.
6. Under managed funds, there is a likelihood of an investor's money being committed to artificially grown agricultural products or artificially enhanced production of poultry and other animals. Food produced in this way is likely to endanger human health. Thus, keep away from such schemes.
7. Avoid the ever-increasing burden of debts. The fictitious and fragile nature of the interest-based system could not have been better expressed than in an article posted on Brookings website that says, "Washington may bail out Wall Street. But who will bail out Washington?" The article discusses the fact that Capitol Hill has been surviving on borrowed time and borrowed money from foreign investors for decades. But can this be long lasting?[427] To prove the point, the author says that in the United States, Medicare alone faces a huge deficit of $36 trillion. The article genuinely expresses the worry

427 Robert L. Bixby et al., 'Rebuild economic confidence by reforming entitlements, *Brookings*, http://www.brookings.edu/research/opinions/2008/11/16-entitlements-sawhill, November 17, 2008.

of every responsible American of not leaving behind a burden of debt on future generations. If foreign investors had reciprocated this worry, then they would have questioned themselves whether the trillions that are pumped or dumped into such a fragile financial system of creating debts in geometric progression, would ever be recovered by their future generations. This is yet another reason why an investor or anybody else should refrain from partaking in this risky game, which is most likely to end up bailing out or paying the price for the blunders of policymakers.

Conclusion

In as much as a word of comfort provides solace to the aggrieved, the subject matter of this book, chapter after chapter, seeks to comfort the hearts of old-aged pensioners and those who have fallen victim to the vagaries of the unpredictable mood of the financial and investment world. This mood fluctuates and swings like a yo-yo, hither and tither, without allowing time and opportunity for innocent members of the public to assimilate and catch up with the erratic development, which eats away their savings and investments as termites eat away wood. Like termites in the world of finance and investment, the speculators, swindlers, and fraudsters get their food supplies from the hard-earned savings and capital of uninformed investors. Yet they turn their trust into misery.

The tragic plight of swindled investors is a nightmare for all decent financial centers in the world. But the headache caused to investors and regulators comes from unregulated offshore financial centers.

Due to phenomenal abuse, there is a wealth of lessons to be learned by regulators and government agencies to trim these offshore centers to size or ban citizens at home from investing in the investment funds registered therein. Perhaps introducing a tax on offshore funds may remedy much of the abuse.

As this book provides essential food for thought to investors, they have to learn to become vigilant and smarter than speculators and swindlers to avoid being abused.

In order to protect their reputation, offshore centers may have to introduce accounting and auditing regulation and mandatory filing requirements, as in onshore centers, even if this causes insomnia to the bosses in large corporations. Heavy fines may have to be levied against noncompliant banks and fund managers.

If members of the public are to be encouraged to participate in economic activities, then they need to be reassured that their lifetime savings will be protected against the collapse of investment schemes. These compensation schemes are becoming common in mainstream financial centers. Similar measures in the form of compensation need to be introduced in offshore centers too.

Glossary of Terms

Ask price

An ask price, also called offer price, offer, asking price, or simply ask, is the price a seller states he or she will accept.

Bid price

A bid price is the highest price that a buyer (i.e., bidder) is willing to pay for a security. It is usually referred to simply as the bid. In bid and ask, the bid price stands in contrast to the ask price or offer, and the difference between the two is called the bid-ask spread. An unsolicited bid or purchase offer is when a person or company receives a bid even though it is not looking to sell.

Boiler room

Literally, where call centers are created, most probably in foreign countries, promoting scam schemes and penny shares.

Boiler room fraud

From business perspective, the term "boiler room" refers to an outbound call center selling questionable investments by telephone. It typically refers to a room where salesmen work using unfair, dishonest sales tactics, sometimes selling penny stocks or private placements or committing outright stock fraud. The term carries a negative connotation, and is often used to imply high-pressure sales tactics and, sometimes, poor working conditions (*Wikipedia*).

Call option

An investing option that confers the right, but not the obligation, to buy a quantity of commodity, currency, stock indices, or financial instruments at a specified price at any time up to a fixed future date

Derivatives

Securities whose values depend on some unknown future events.

Earned income

Earned income is income derived from active participation in a trade or business, including wages, salary, tips, commissions, and bonuses. This is the opposite of unearned income.

Flutter

Chiefly British: a small wager or speculative investment.

Gearing

Gearing means converting shareholders' equity into loan stock, where fixed interest payable on loan stock becomes a charge against profit.

Hedge funds

Funds that allow fund managers to "hedge their bets," with the objective of controlling risk.

Insider trading

Management's use of privileged information.

Intrinsic value

The price of a traded option whose value is calculated as the market price minus the exercise price.

Investment trust

A limited company whose business is the investment of shareholders' funds, the shares being traded like those of any other public company.

Junk bonds

Any corporate bonds with a low rating and a high yield, often involving high risk.

Money laundering

Transferring illegally obtained money or investments through an outside party to conceal the true source.

Noise in the market

The market activity that results when investors base their investment decisions solely on price movements.

Offshore funds

Funds sold under very attractive ventures in which conmen may get their shady schemes registered in offshore centers to escape any legal accountability and controls.

P/E or price-earnings ratio

P/E ratio or price-to-earnings ratio is an essential stock market measure. To calculate a P/E ratio, one simply divides a company's current share price by its latest or predicted earnings per share (EPS). EPS is the slice of the company's after-tax profits every year.

Portfolio theory

A theory that advocates diversification or an asset mix, urging investors to ignore short-term market swings and stay with the market on a long-term basis.

Pump-and-dump

Literally, Pump-and-dump (P&D) is a form of microcap stock fraud that involves artificially inflating the price of an owned stock through false and misleading positive statements, in order to sell the cheaply purchased stock at a higher price. Once the operators of the scheme sell their overvalued shares, the price falls, and investors lose their money. Stocks that are the subject of P&D schemes are sometimes called "chop stocks" (*Wikipedia*).

Pump-and-dump penny stocks

In terms of investment, stocks created when promoters buy a huge quantity of penny shares and then sell them at highly inflated prices.

Punter

In UK a person who gambles (risks money guessing the result of something).

Put option

An investing option that confers the right, but not the obligation, to sell a quantity of commodity, currency, stock indices, or financial instruments at a specified price before a fixed future date.

Pyramid scheme

A scheme in which a fraudster uses money supplied by subscribers to pay off earlier subscribers, with a guaranteed amount being paid to him upon the addition of each subscriber.

Risk spreading

This is the concept that limits loss or potential losses by avoiding to expose the entire portfolio to risky investment.

S&P 500 index

Standard & Poor's market capitalization–weighted index of the five hundred most commonly held stocks.

Share-capital account

Capital stock (in US English) refers to the portion of a company's equity that has been obtained by trading stock to a shareholder for cash. In its strict sense, as used in accounting, share capital comprises the nominal values of all shares issued (that is, the sum of their par values, as printed on the share certificates).

Share-premium account

A share-premium account is typically listed on a company's balance sheet. This account is credited with money paid, or promised to be paid, by a shareholder for a share but only when the shareholder pays more than the cost of a share. This account can be used to write off equity-related expenses, such as underwriting costs, and may also be used to issue bonus shares.

Speculation

The process through which a short-term position is taken in the market with a view of making a quick gain.

Spread betting

Spread betting is a type of speculation that involves taking a bet on the price movement of a security. A spread betting company quotes two prices, the bid and offer price (also called the spread), and investors bet whether the price of the underlying stock will be lower than the bid or higher than the offer. Investors do not own the underlying stock in spread betting; they simply speculate on the price movement of the stock.

Stagging

The purchase of shares in new issues, with the purpose of selling them at a profit on the commencement of dealings.

Stock market

A market for buying and selling stocks and shares of publicly listed companies.

Third-generation (3G) mobile telecommunications

The impact of technological change on mobile telecommunications is often described in terms of generations. Thus, first-generation mobile technology refers to the analogue cellular systems that characterized the 1980s and early 1990s, while second generation refers to today's digital cellular systems, such as the widely used Global System for Mobile Communications (GSM). So-called third-generation (3G) systems or IMT-2000 include high-speed data, mobile Internet access, and entertainment such as games, music, and video programs using image, video, and sound to mobile users ("Licensing of Third Generation (3G) Mobile Briefing paper," https://www.itu.int/osg/spu/ni/3G/workshop/Briefing_paper.PDF).

Time value

A premium over intrinsic value.

Unearned income

Unearned income describes any personal income that comes from investments and other sources unrelated to employment services. Examples of unearned income include interest from a savings account, bond interest, alimony, and dividends from stock. This type of income differs from traditionally earned income, which is the income earned from active work or business activity (*Investopedia*).

Unit trust

A trust formed to manage a portfolio of stock exchange securities, in which small investors can buy units.

Bibliography

Books

Adams, J. R., and D. Frantz. *A Full-Service Bank: How BCCI Stole Billions around the World*. London: Simon & Schuster, 1992.

Bales, K. *Disposable People: New Slavery in the Global Economy*. California: University of California Press, 1999.

Beckman, R. *Crashes: Why They Happen, What to Do*. London: Sidgwick and Jackson, 1988.

Foster, John Bellamy, and Fred Magdoff. *The Great Financial Crisis: Causes and Consequences*. New York: Monthly Review Press, 2009.

Bose, M. *The Crash*. London: Bloomsbury Publishing, 1988.

Bower, T. *Maxwell: The Final Verdict*. London: HarperCollins Publishers, 1995.

Blustein, Paul. *The Chastening: Inside the Crisis That Rocked the Global Financial System and Humbled the IMF*. Oxford: Public Affairs, 2001.

Chapman, C. *How the Stock Markets Work: A Guide to the International Markets*, 6th ed. London: Century Ltd., 1998.

Davis, J. *Money Makers: The Stock Market Secrets of Britain's Top Professional Investors*. London: Orion Publishing Group, 1998.

Engler, A. *Apostles of Greed: Capitalism and the Myth of the Individual in the Market*. London & Colorado: Pluto Press, 1995, and Nova Scotia (Canada): Fernwood Publishing, 1995.

Galbraith, J. K. *The Great Crash of 1929*. Middlesex: Penguin Books, 1979.

Geisst, C. R. *Wall Street: A History*. New York and Oxford: Oxford University Press, 1997.

Golding, Tony. *The City inside the Great Expectation Machine*, 2nd ed. London: Financial Times, 2003.

Haugen, Robert A. *The Inefficient Stock Market*. New Jersey: Prentice Hall, 1999.

Heller, Robert. *The Naked Investor*. London: Weidenfeld & Nicolson, 1976.

The Hutchinson Encyclopedia, 3rd ed. Middlesex: Helicon Publishing, 1996.

Jacobs, B. I. *Capital Ideas and Market Realities: Option Replication, Investor Behavior, and Stock Market Crashes*. Malden, Massachusetts and Oxford: Blackwell Publishers, 1999.

Johnson, H. J. *Global Financial Institutions and Markets*. Malden, Massachusetts and Oxford: Blackwell Publishers, 2000.

Kamali, Muhammad Hashim. *Islamic Commercial Law: An Analysis of Futures and Options*. I. B. Tauris and the Islamic Text Society, Cambridge, 2001.

Mackay, C. *Extraordinary Popular Delusions and the Madness of Crowds*. Hertfordshire: Wandsworth, 1995.

Mercer, D. (ed.). *Chronicle of the Twentieth Century*. Paris: Jacques Legrand, and London: Chronicle Communications, 1988.

Mitchell, Kennedy. *Single Stock Futures: An Investor's Guide*. New Jersey: John Wiley & Sons, 2003.

Morris, C. R. *Money, Greed, and Risk: Why Financial Crises and Crashes Happen*. West Sussex: John Wiley & Sons, 1999.

The New Book of Knowledge, vol. 17. Connecticut: Grolier Inc., 1996.

Samuels J. M., and F. M. Wilkes. *Management of Company Finance*, 2nd ed. London: Thomas Nelson & Sons, 1975.

Soros, George. *The Crash of 2008 and What It Means*. New York: Public Affairs, 2009.

Stewart, T. H. *How Charts Can Make You Money: Technical Analysis for Investors*, 4th ed. Cambridge: Woodhead-Faulkner, and New York: Nichols Publishing, 1986.

Strange, Susan. *Casino Capitalism*. Manchester: Manchester University Press, and New York: St. Martin's Press, 1997.

Thomas, G., and M. Morgan-Witts. *The Day the Bubble Burst: A Social History of the Wall Street Crash*. London: Hamish Hamilton, 1979.

Walters, M. *How to Make a Killing in the Share Jungle*, 6th ed. London and Virginia: B. T. Batsford, 1998.

Warburton, P. *Debt and Delusion*. London and New York: Allen Lane/Penguin Press, 1999.

Wilson, R. (ed.). *Islamic Financial Market*. London and New York: Routledge, 1998.

Wood, C. *Boom and Bust*. London: Sidgwick and Jackson, 1988.

Newspapers, Magazines, and Journals

ACCA Corporate sector Review

Michelle Perry, "Share Options," Corporate Sector Review, ACCA, issue 42, October 2002.

Colin Coulson-Thomas, "Communicating Success," Corporate Sector Review, ACCA, issue 42, October 2002.

Al-Hayat daily Arabic news,
Issue No. 11031, April 26, 1993, news on the closure of BCCI.

Arab News
Mahmood Rafique, "Financial Frauds Cost Billions of Dollars in Losses: Poll," *Arab News*, October 23, 2008.

Business.com
"The 1929 Stock Market Crash," University of Melbourne, Business.com, http://www.arts.unimelb.edu.au/amu/ucr/. (n.d.) (converted into digitalized collection).
"The 1987 Stock Market Crash," University of Melbourne, Business.com, http://www.arts.unimelb.edu.au/amu/ucr/. (n.d.) (converted into digitalized collection).
Jim Jubak, "96/10—Crash Testing," www.Business.com, October 1996. (converted into digitalized collection).

Business Standard
'Coke, Oracle, Intel use Cayman Islands to avoid US taxes,' *Business Standard*, http://www.business-standard.com/article/companies/coke-oracle-intel-use-cayman-islands-to-avoid-us-taxes-109050600023_1.html, *May 6, 2009.*

Daily Reckoning, Paris, November 27, 2002.
Porter Stansberry, "The Debt Generation," *Daily Reckoning*, Paris, November 27, 2002.

Financial Times
"Leader: Trouble in Tokyo," Financial Times, October 25, 2002.

Harvey Morris, "'Asian Crash' Case Accused Wins Fight to Stay in UK," *Financial Times*, July 28, 2001.

Financial Times, http://financialtimes.Printthis.Clickability.com, http://news.ft.com/servlet/ContentServer, and http://specials.ft.com/.

'Pell quits RBS with £9.8m pension', *Financial Times*, http://www.ft.com/cms/s/0/24737b06-3a9f-11de-8a2d-00144feabdc0.html#axzz4FQ1nHvlz, May 7, 2009.

Tony Tassell, "Executive Pay 'Still Not Made Clear to Investors,'" *Financial Times*, November 27, 2002.

Peter Thal Larsen, "Court Report Sheds Light on WorldCom's Ways," *Financial Times*, November 5, 2002.

Barry Riley, "FT Fund Management: Preparing for the Upturn," *Financial Times*, October 17, 2002.

William Barnes, et al., "Boiler-Room Problem Is Spreading across Asia," *Financial Times*, July 29, 2001.

Focus 21, Al-Nahdah, no. 1 (2001).

Islamic Financial Institutions. Seminar Proceedings Series no. 27. Jeddah (Saudi Arabia): Islamic Development Bank, 1995.

Islamic Futures and Their Markets. Research paper no. 32. Jeddah (Saudi Arabia): Islamic Development Bank, Islamic Research and Training Institute, 1995.

Issues in Islamic Banking: Selected Papers. Leicester (UK): The Islamic Foundation, 1994.

FT com:

Andrew Hill, "Rethinking Rockefeller and the Rest," *FT.com*, http://financialtimes.Printthis.Clickability.com, July 30, 2002,

John Thornhill, "Corporate Restructuring: Fat Cats Go on a Diet," *FT.com*, October 17, 2002.

Caroline Daniel, "Insiders Who Managed to Get Out Just in Time," FT.com, July 31, 2002, http://news.ft.com/servlet/ContentServer.

Ien Cheng, "Survivors Who Laughed All the Way to the Bank," FT.com, July 30, 2002, http://financialtimes.printthis.clickability.com.

Ien Cheng, "Executives in Top US Collapse Made $3.3bn," FT.com, July 30, 2002, http://financialtimes.printthis.clickability.com.

Andrew Hill and Peter Spiegal, "Feeling the Heat," FT.com, May 9, 2002, http://news.ft.com/servlet/ContentServer.

Peter Spiegel, "Andersen Parent Agrees $60m Enron Payout," FT.com, August 27, 2002, http://news.ft.com/servlet/ContentServer.

Peter Spiegel, "Former Enron Executive Pleads Guilty to Fraud Charges," FT.com, August 22, 2002, http://news.ft.com/servlet/ContentServer.

Peter Spiegel, "NatWest Bankers Indicted for Enron Role," FT.com, September 13, 2002, http://news.ft.com/Servlet/ContentServer.

Lina Saigol, "Lavish, Laddish and the Lure of Lucrative Fee," FT.com, June 29, 2002, http://news.ft.com/servlet/ContenServer.

"After Enron—Agenda for Reform 2002—Unofficial Watchdogs Need Sharper Eyesight," FT.com, February 14, 2002, http://specials.ft.com/afr2002/FT.

"Enron: Who's Investigating Whom?" FT.com, January 18, 2002, http://news.ft.com/ft/gx.cgi/ftc.

Stephen Kirchgaessner and Peter Thal Larsen, "Life under Watchful Eye of Ebbers," FT.com, August 25, 2002, http://news.ft.com/servlet/ContentServer, accessed on September 15, 2002.

Lina Saigol, "Spinning a Web for the City Regulators to Unravel," FT.com, October 24, 2002.

Peter Thal Larsen, "The Job of Salvage Set to Begin," FT.com, July 22, 2002, http://news.ft.com/servlet/ContentServer.

Mail Online

'The building in tax haven that 20,000 firms call home: Cayman Islands has more companies than inhabitants', *Mail Online, http://www.dailymail.co.uk/news/article-3411183/The-building-tax-haven-20-000-firms-call-home-Cayman-Islands-companies-registered-inhabitants.html, January* 22, *2016.*

Sam Fleming, 'Greed that fuelled the crash: How city fat cats took home £17bn bonuses... as their banks crumbled', *Mail Online*, http://www.dailymail.co.uk/news/article-1077120/Greed-fuelled-crash-How-city-fat-cats-took-home-17bn-bonuses--banks-crumbled.html, 14 October, 2008.

New Internationalist

Melissa Benn, "How to Make Dirty Money Squeaky Clean," *New Internationalist*, issue 224, October 1991.

Review of Islamic Economics. No. 9. Leicester (UK): International Association for Islamic Economics and the Islamic Foundation, 2000.

Observer

"Downfall of an $80bn Firm," Observer, January 13, 2002, http://www.guardian.co.uk/enron/story.

Review of Islamic Economics

Khurshid Ahmad, "Islamic Finance and Banking: The Challenge and Prospects," in Review of Islamic Economics (2000), 70, quoting Economist, May 30, 1998.

The Telegraph

"Financial crisis is 'man-made catastrophe'", says World Bank chief, *The Telegraph*, http://www.telegraph.co.uk/finance/financialcrisis/3187467/Financial-crisis-is-man-made-catastrophe-says-World-Bank-chief.html, 13 October, 2008.

Bank of England statement in full, *The Telegraph*, http://www.telegraph.co.uk/finance/personalfinance/interest-rates/3391011/Bank-of-England-statement-in-full.html, 6 November, 2008.

USA Today:

Jeffrey Stinson, 'Victims of Madoff's alleged Wall Street scam spread to Europe', *USA Today*, http://abcnews.go.com/Business/story?id=6467617&page=1, n.d.

Wall Street Journal:

'Victims react to Madoff's sentencing', Wall Street Journal video, http://www.wsj.com/video/victims-react-to-madoff-sentencing/541815EA-1FB9-4F05-B620-6ABFFB267029.html, 29 June, 2009.

Internet Sites

AccountancyAge.com

Duncan Hughes, "Now the Fed Enters Standards Battle," AccountancyAge.com, July 25, 2002, http://www.accountancyage.com/Analysis/.

Al Jazeera (Arabic TV news from Qatar), August 22, 2002. (regarding total Saudi investments in the U.S.)

ANN (Arabic TV news from the UK), September 22, 2002 (regarding total Arab investments in the U.S.)

Associated Press

John Leicester, "France Telecom Posts $12B Loss," *Associated Press*, September 13, 2002, http://Story.news.yahoo.com/news.

Baltimore Technologies, http://www.baltimore.com/news/press/.

BBC News, http://news.bbc.co.uk/.

'Bank of America bail-out agreed', *BBC News*, http://news.bbc.co.uk/1/hi/business/7832484.stm, January 16, 2009.

"Stanfold Charged with Fraud in US," *BBC News*, http://news.bbc.co.uk/1/hi/world/americas/8109690.stm., 19 June, 2009.

'Pension regulator warns on fraud', *BBC-news*, http://news.bbc.co.uk/1/hi/business/8007674.stm, 20 April. 2009.

"Germany Plans Mobilcom Rescue," BBC News, September 13, 2002, http://news.bbc.co.uk/2/hi/business/.

BBC 1 and 2:

Panorama: "The Six Billion Dollar Man," *BBC 1*, May 11, 2009.

"Credit Crash Britain Money for Nothing," BBC money program, *BBC 2*, http://www.bbc.co.uk/programmes/b00fcvrl, November 6, 2008.

Bloomberg:

Jon Menon and Charles Penty, "Madoff's 'Lie' Ensnares Victims From Paris to Tokyo", *Bloomberg*, http://www.canadianhedgewatch.com/content/news/general/?id=3875, 15 December, 2008.

Brookings,

Robert L. Bixby et al., 'Rebuild economic confidence by reforming entitlements, Brookings, http://www.brookings.edu/research/opinions/2008/11/16-entitlements-sawhill, November 17,, 2008.

City of London Police

"International Police Operation Targets Suspected Boiler Room Masterminds." City of London Police, April 3, 2014, https://www.cityoflondon.police.uk/news-and-appeals/international-police-operation-targets-suspected-boiler-room-masterminds.

DW Mode for Minds

"Deutsche Telecom Chief Steps Down," DW Mode for Minds (editorial), July 16, 2002 http://www.dw-world.de/dw/article/0,1431,593333,00.html, accessed July 16, 2002.

Empower America, http://www.empoweramerica.org/stories.

Fox News, http://www.foxnews.com/us/ and http://www.foxnews.com/story/.

Financial Mail on Sunday:

'Former RBS boss Stephen Hester set for £500,000 payout from bailed-out bank - more than two years after he left', *Financial Mail on Sunday*, http://www.thisismoney.co.uk/money/news/article-3435249/Former-Royal-Bank-Scotland-boss-Stephen-Hester-course-final-payout-bailed-organisation-500000-two-years-left.html#ixzz4EhCFJU00, 6 February, 2016.

Financial Services Authority

"FCA Campaigns to Protect Public from Investment Fraud," Financial Services Authority, May 26, 2016, http://www.fscs.org.uk/news/2016/may/fca-campaign-to-protect-public-from-investment-fraud/.

"Unauthorised Overseas Firms Operating in the UK," Financial Services Authority website, http://www.fsa.gov.uk/pages/Doing/Regulated/Law/Alerts/overseas.shtml.

Guardian, http://www.guardian.co.uk/.

Pres conference, https://www.theguardian.com/business/2008/oct/13/markettur-moil-creditcrunch, 13 October, 2008.

'State-supported investment banks set billions aside for bonuses', *The Guardian*, https://www.theguardian.com/business/2008/nov/03/european-bank-bonuses-executive-salaries, November 3, 2008.

PatrickWintour and Audrey Gillan. 'Lost in Iceland: £1 billion from councils, charities and police', *The Guardian*, https://www.theguardian.com/business/2008/oct/10/banking-iceland, 10 October, 2008.

Ashley Seager et al., 'Shock as Bank of England slashes rate to 3%, *The Guardian*, https://www.theguardian.com/business/2008/nov/06/interestrates-interestrates2, November 6, 2008.

David Teather, "Duncan Denies Ordering Enron Shredding," *The Guardian*, May 18, 2002, http://www.guardian.co.uk/enron/story.

"Bush Urges 'New Era of Integrity,'" *The Guardian*, July 9, 2002, http://www.guardian.co.uk/bush/story.

"Bush on Back Foot over Corporate Past," *The Guardian*, July 2002, http://www.guardian.co.uk/enron/story/.

Paul Krugman, "How Bush Firm Used Accounting Scam," *The Guardian*, July 9, 2002, http://www.guardian.co.uk/enron/story/.

Mark Tran, "Enron Admits Spending $2.5m on Lobbying," *The Guardian*, March 8, 2002, http://www.guardian.co.uk/enron/story/.

David Teather, "FBI Investigates Army Secretary's Enron Dealings," *The Guardian*, April 16, 2002, http://www.guardian.co.uk/enron/story/.

David Teather, "White House Faces Subpoena," *The Guardian*, May 23, 2002, http://www.guardian.co.uk/enron/stories.

"Special Reports Enron: Web of Intrigue," Guardian, http://www.guardian.co.uk/flash/.

Madeleine Bunting, "Fall of the arrogant", Special Reports Enron: Web of Intrigue, The Guardian, Jan. 22, 2002.

"Enron," *The Guardian*, January 31, 2002, http://www.guardian.co.uk/enron.story/.

Jill Treanor, "Banks 'Knew of Enron Scam,'" *The Guardian*, July 24, 2002, http://www.guardian.co.uk/Archive/Article.

"I Was a Teenage Fraudster," *The Guardian*, July 11, 2002, http://www.guardian.co.uk/worldcom.story.

Mark Tran, "WorldCom Goes Bankrupt," *The Guardian*, July 22, 2002, ttp://www.guardian.co.uk/Archive/Article/.

David Teather, "$4bn US Fraud Scandal Sparks Market Turmoil," *The Guardian*, June 27, 2002, http://www.guardian.co.uk/Archive/Article/, accessed on July 24, 2002.

Jill Treanor, "$40bn in Debt—and Counting," *The Guardian*, July 23, 2002, http://www.guardian.co.uk/worldcom/story/.

Neil Hume, et al., "FTSE Closes Down below 4,000 as Bush Intervention Fails," *The Guardian*, July 16, 2002, http://www.guardian.co.uk/bush/story/.

Holland and Knight

Eugene M. Propper, "International Corporate Fraud Investigations," Holland & Knight, March 16, 2000, http://www.hklaw.com/OtherPublication, accessed on October 26, 2002.

Independent (The British newspaper)

'RBS chief Stephen Hester set for £9.6m incentive package', *Independent*, http://www.independent.co.uk/news/business/news/rbs-chief-stephen-hester-set-for-pound96m-incentive-package-1712427.html, 22 June, 2009.

David Usborne, "Wall St. Brokers Reduced Life Savings of £490,000 to £282," *Independent*, July 23, 2001.

International Monetary Fund annual report 2009, https://www.imf.org/external/pubs/ft/ar/2009/eng/pdf/ar09_eng.pdf.

Journal of Economics and Business

William O. Brown Jr. and Richard C. K. Burdekin, "Fraud and Financial Markets: The 1997 Collapse of the Junior Mining Stocks," Claremont College (California), http://ideas.repec.org/s/clm/clmeco.html. Journal of Economics and Business, Vol. 52, Issue 3, May – June 2000.

'Justice delayed: The Ombudsman's House of Commons Public Administration Second Report on Equitable Life, http://www.publications.parliament.uk/pa/cm200809/cmselect/cmpubadm/41/41i.pdf, 11 December, 2008.

The Motley Fool:

Patrick Morris, 'Warren Buffett Tells You the Difference Between Stock Trading and Investing', The Motley Fool, http://www.fool.com/investing/general/2014/12/14/warren-buffett-tells-you-the-difference-between-st.aspx, 14 December, 2014.

Politics.co.uk. http://www.politics.co.uk/news/2009/5/1/

"Banks 'author of their own demise' ", politics.co.uk, http://www.politics.co.uk/news/2009/5/1/banks-authors-of-their-own-demise 1 May, 2009.

Reuters, http://today.reuters.com/news/.

Tokyo Stock Exchange history, http://www.tse.or.jp/english/about/history.html. 19 Feb. 2013.

Treasury's Small Quoted Companies' report

"Tomorrow's Giants," February 1999, a sequel to the Treasury's Small Quoted Companies report published in November 1998.

US Department of State, http://usinfo.state.gov/topical/global/drugs/01020501.htm.

Washington Post

Christopher Stern, "Telecom Slump Continues," *Washington Post*, September 14, 2002, http://www.washington/post.com/wp-dyn/.

Wikipedia Encyclopedia

Irving Fisher, *Wikipedia Encyclopedia*, https://en.wikipedia.org/wiki/Irving_Fisher.

Boiler room business, *Wikipedia Encyclopedia*, https://en.wikipedia.org/wiki/Boiler_room_(business)

http://en.wikipedia.org/wiki/Deutsche_Telekom.

Wiki News

'Market maker Bernard L. Madoff arrested in $50B 'giant Ponzi scheme', *Wiki News*, https://en.wikinews.org/wiki/Market_maker_Bernard_L._Madoff_arrested_in_$50B_%27giant_Ponzi_scheme%27, 12 December, 2008..

Index

65691572R00105

Made in the USA
Charleston, SC
05 January 2017